FRANCES ELKINS

VISIONARY AMERICAN DESIGNER

SCOTT POWELL

Rizzoli
NEW YORK

New York · Paris · London · Milan

CONTENTS

FRANCES ELKINS

FOUNDING A STYLE

IN NAMING THE STRONGEST influences on evolving his own work, Billy Baldwin— arguably the most influential American interior designer of the second half of the twentieth century—first cites Elsie de Wolfe, who founded the profession. However, he reserves his highest praise for someone whose reputation is still only partially valued at its true worth. "Frances Elkins was the most creative decorator we ever had, and perhaps the greatest," he asserted. The superbly crafted work of Frances Adler Elkins (1888–1953) has few peers in legitimately garnering the title "timeless."

Working primarily in California and in the environs of Chicago and New York, Frances carried out a wide range of commissions and collaborations for houses, hotels, offices, and country clubs from Honolulu to Long Island. Beginning in the 1920s and continuing into the mid-1950s, Frances was known for creating exquisitely beautiful rooms with an inviting sense of comfort.

Her work was significant for several reasons. She was the first to gracefully blend classical elements with the cutting edge of contemporary Parisian furniture and interior design. She had a perfect sense of scale and balance. Her color sense was superb. And she was one of the most knowledgeable decorators of her period about not only traditional French and English furniture, but about historic and on-the-cusp-of-the-moment textiles and wall coverings. Her vision also encompassed the decorative arts of Asia, and of Mexico in her later work.

Many of her most renowned interiors were in houses designed by her famous brother, David Adler. Schooled at the École des Beaux Arts in Paris, Adler first instilled in his sister an unwavering respect for classical proportion, symmetry, and harmony. This disciplined approach was the solid foundation for all of Frances's compositions, no matter how up-to-the-minute or boldly colored. Like Frances, he inserted contemporary accents into what may have been the finest American classical house architecture of the twentieth century. An example is the banister of ebony atop glass spindles in the late-eighteenth-century Classical-style staircase for Mrs. Kersey Coates Reed's house in Lake Forest, Illinois (1929–32). Equally elegant was the entrance hall for Mrs. Evelyn Marshall's

OPPOSITE Frances Elkins, portrait by
Eugene Hutchinson, circa 1925.

FRANCES ELKINS *VISIONARY AMERICAN DESIGNER*

house on Long Island (1931–34) with flooring of ebonized oak banded with geometric steel inlays, in a design inspired by antiquity. This Art Moderne element supports a Roman arched colonnade in traditional wood and plaster.

Well-traveled and always running in the highest social and artistic circles, Frances was blessed with a uniquely rich range of influences and opportunities, which allowed her to create an international eclecticism unparalleled in her day. Known for her vital associations with European style icons and trend-setters such as Jean-Michel Frank, Alberto Giacometti, Salvador Dalí, and Coco Chanel, Frances earned an international reputation among her peers as the most imaginative and innovative interior designer of her time. Billy Baldwin called Frank "genius of French furniture," and it was Frances who had introduced him and his work to the United States. Not to be underestimated was the importance of Elkins's introduction to the United States of his work and style in avant-garde furniture and interior design.

Beginning with a story on Casa Amesti, her Monterey home, in what was then known as *The House Beautiful*, in 1924, national publications including *House & Garden*, *Town & Country*, *Vogue*, *Harper's Bazaar*, and *Arts & Decoration* presented her work with a greater frequency than is remembered today. This coverage was augmented by widespread newspaper reportage, particularly in the California and Chicago press.

What gave her rooms great vitality was Frances's masterful use of contrast—contrasts of colors, textures, and historical periods, seamlessly integrated, and for the first time in the history of interior design, a deliberate and deft mixture of the luxurious with the humble. Nonetheless, in all of her interiors there was a wonderful simplicity and subtlety. The materials and finishes were always first-rate. She often seasoned her designs with exotic or fanciful elements, knowing such flourishes would delight the eye.

Alongside her signature combinations of bold colors, Frances could be equally effective with a subdued color palette, or, uniquely to her own work, the juxtaposition of both. Older as well as newly commissioned color photos allow us to appreciate her consummate finesse with color.

Design historian Stanley Barrows, for twenty years director of the Interior Design Department at the Parsons School, and later chairman of the Interior Design Department at the Fashion Institute of Technology, would often praise Elkins's particular gift with texture. The outstanding textural balance of Elkins's rooms can also be easily discerned in many newly available photographs.

As can now be shown, many of the world's most famous photographers captured her rooms—Ansel Adams, Julius Shulman, Maynard Parker, Yousuf Karsh, André Kertész, Louise Dahl-Wolfe, Cecil Beaton, Fred Lyon, Emelie Danielson, George Hoyningen-Huene, Karen Radkai, and Slim Aarons, just for starters.

In addition to achieving visual balance through a very architectural sense of furniture planning, Frances was also known for comfort and convenience. Her rooms worked well for both men and women, with sturdy upholstered furniture, durable fabrics, and spacious floor plans, and much care given to the useful placement of lamps, end tables, bookcases, and storage.

In her thirty-plus-year career, Frances achieved a level of inspired perfection that has recently earned her an almost cultlike following. This renewed interest began with Stephen Salny's 1980 article on Frances and the Mrs. Kersey Coates Reed house in *Architectural Digest*. Further awareness of Frances's importance was raised by Dupuy Warrick Reed's 1984 *Connoisseur* magazine profile, Lois Wagner Green's 1988 article in *Interior Design*, Diane Dorrans Saeks's story in *Pebble Beach* magazine, Penelope Rowlands 1998 *AD* article on Casa Amesti, Elkins's Monterey home, and Pauline Metcalf's essay on Elkins in *David Adler: The Elements of Style* (2002). The Elkins reawakening (rebirth / revival / resurgence) culminated in the first monograph on the subject, Stephen Salny's *Frances Elkins:*

OPPOSITE Entry hall, Evelyn Marshall Field residence (Syosset, New York), with ebonized floor banded in steel inlay, 1935.

ABOVE *House Beautiful* cover, June 1949, featuring the lanai from the George Coleman, Jr. residence (Pebble Beach, California).

Interior Design (2005). Today, Frances and her furniture designs are often referenced in print media in articles on newly decorated rooms, and online in numerous design blogs. Thomas Jayne's 2010 book, *The Finest Rooms in America: 50 Influential Interiors from the 18th Century to the Present*, featured Frances's Casa Amesti drawing room. Jennifer Boles incorporated a chapter on Frances in her 2018 book, *Inspired Design: The 100 Most Important Designers of the Past 100 Years*, illustrated with a photo of the celebrated library in the Mrs. Kersey Coates Reed house. Phaidon Press included Elkins in its 2019 book, *Interiors: The Greatest Rooms of the 20th Century*, featuring the library in the Leslie Wheeler house in Lake Forest, Illinois. There is now a burgeoning focus on the individual components that combine to give her designs a vibrant freshness that has stood the test of time.

In service of this aim, a wealth of verbal and visual material has recently come to light, which enables us to even more firmly examine her achievements at a greater level of detail than ever before possible. Similarly reawakened today is the investigation of her importance not only in the field of interior design but also in furniture and textile design, achievements that can now be fully illustrated. Her collaboration with California weaver Dorothy Liebes in the second half of her career put Frances at the vanguard of a revolution in American textile design. What can also now be understood is the extent of her close collaborations with no less than ten distinguished architects in addition to her brother. Prominent among them were Gardner Dailey, William Wurster, Clarence Tantau, George Washington Smith, and Wallace Neff.

This diversity of new information not only reveals her astoundingly prolific output but also what inspired Frances to create rooms of such distinction. Materials from her recently located project files and personal archives contain previously unknown letters, drawings, and other important documents. Also included are samples of fabrics and wall coverings used in her designs, combined with many examples from her private collection of distinctive table and household linens. A plethora of historic images of not only her rooms but also their individual furnishings

and accessories help chart the trajectory of the remarkable breadth of her career. An especially revealing glimpse of the development of her own style can be gleaned from her twelve red-leather-bound inspiration scrapbooks.

Though primarily a design chronicle, the pages that follow also offer social history, incorporating historic photographs from newspaper and magazine archives as well as family collections. These images provide an extraordinary window into how Elkins's private and commercial interiors were an ultrasmart backdrop for the busy lives of her high-society clients, Hollywood stars, soldiers, college students, and the general public in California, the North Shore Chicago suburbs, New York, Hawaii, and elsewhere. Images of Frances's collaborators as well as workers in her large Monterey operation pay tribute to the team who helped her produce work of such quality.

With her refined sensibility and educated eye, Frances was able to develop "a new American style." Mark Hampton, who praised Elkins's "clean, fresh look," and her singular ability among American designers to incorporate an "element of glamour," noted that she "synthesized different styles in a way that was typically American but which went beyond anything else done at the time."

On the subject of a new American style, Frances told *What's Doing* magazine in 1946, "I have always felt equally strongly that we should use our own creative force to express our own era. I felt that, as our needs were

ABOVE 1934 Exterior rendering by the office of David Adler of Mrs. J. Ogden Armour residence (Lake Forest Illinois). As an unusual "couture" detail, Adler designed removable wooden Venetian blinds to hang *outside* the windows in warmer weather.

OPPOSITE BOTTOM Breakfast room, Sidney Ehrman residence (San Francisco, California), decorated circa 1940s. Chippendale tables and chairs, a Hepplewhite breakfront, Chinese rug, an antique Chinese mural, and Ming Dynasty jar were part of the decor.

David Adler-Architect.

different, we should liberate ourselves from European ideas and spirit and design articles suitable to our way of life."

As perhaps her most ardent follower, the late interior designer Michael Taylor asserts that Frances Elkins was "vastly underplayed" in relation to Elsie de Wolfe and Syrie Maugham. Elkins was the one "pure genius" among the three pioneering women decorators. Timing is everything. Taylor emphasized that "[h]er genius was in doing it *when she did*."

In summing up her lasting influence on the entire profession, Los Angeles–based interior designer Michael S. Smith says, "Her work is chic, full of superb craftsmanship, worldly, understated, timeless. You could walk into

even her grandest rooms today and feel very much at home. They still look modern sixty years later." •

OPPOSITE Grand staircase, Mrs. Kersey Coates Reed residence (Lake Forest, Illinois), 1929–1932, with Steuben-glass balusters, ebony handrail, crystal chandelier, and black-and-white marble floor.

ABOVE Dining room, Mrs. Van Horn Ely Sr. residence (Haverford, Pennsylvania), decorated circa 1937. The room decor includes Frances's iconic "loop" chairs; Serge Roche furniture, including mirrored obelisks; Baguès wall lights; and black floor with white-marble inserts. The entire room, shown in 1951, was possibly moved and reinstalled circa 1950 with the aid of decorator Jesse Earnshaw.

THE EARLY YEARS

What made Frances Elkins Frances Elkins? *What transformed a Jewish society belle from the Midwest into possibly the most original of all American interior designers?*

FRANCES'S LIFE SPANNED a remarkable arc of world history, beginning in booming Victorian Milwaukee in 1888—at a time when the Queen Anne style of architecture was considered fashionable among wealthy Americans—and ending in San Francisco in 1953, at the dawn of the Jet Age.[1]

Several key influences on young Frances's creative sensibility have been firmly established: One key defining factor was the role Therese Adler, Frances's mother, had in her daughter's broad education, including trips to Europe and sending Frances to boarding schools in France, Italy, and Switzerland.

In his chapter on Frances in *The Great Lady Decorators*, Adam Lewis supports this, writing that "Therese had both the money and the leisure time needed to make extended trips abroad with her children. For years, they made prolonged excursions to all of the great cities of Europe, where David and Frances were steeped in learning about neoclassical architecture, the history of the French and Italian Renaissances, and the arts of eighteenth-century France and England. These trips instilled in Frances a never-ending love for the cities of Paris and Venice."

Another big influence was the guiding hand of her artistic older brother, David Adler Jr., who was to become perhaps the most innovative and imaginative architect of American classical houses in the first half of the 20th century. David's architecture studies at the École des Beaux-Arts in Paris, which he imparted to Frances, provided an enduring historical foundation for both siblings to attain their mature style, with its strong emphasis on scale, proportion, and meticulous detail. And, lastly, the cultivated environment of late-19th-century and early-20th-century Milwaukee, which was dominated by German immigrants and their descendants, also left its mark on Frances.

ABOVE Prospect Avenue, circa 1900, with the Adler double houses with "witches hat" roofs on the turrets, second from right. This block view shows relatively modest homes compared to the palatial Victorian castles on other parts of the avenue.

OPPOSITE, CLOCKWISE FROM TOP The side-by-side Adler family homes at 173 and 175 Prospect Avenue in an artist's rendering from a period photo. Frances lived at 175 from 1887 to 1918, nearly half of her life. Bottom right: A coachman outside the Pillsbury mansion on Prospect Avenue, circa 1903. Bottom left: Therese Adler with Fannie, circa 1893.

In the mid-1850s, Midwestern cities began attracting massive numbers of Jews emigrating from Eastern Europe. German Jews like Frances's grandparents became American success stories, prospering in trade, manufacturing, banking, and other professions.

In *Magnificent Milwaukee*, architectural historian Russell Zimmerman illuminates the qualities that made Milwaukee not only a manufacturing center but also a cultural one, partly from the influence of its many German immigrants, many of whom were "architects and craftsmen [who] could not help but leave a strong imprint on Milwaukee."

Responding to anti-Semitic snobbery, affluent German-American Jews at the time established their own closed societies akin to New York City's elite Four Hundred, what Stephen Birmingham in *Our Crowd: The Great Jewish Families of New York* called "the closest thing to aristocracy that the country had seen."

The Adler family fortune continued to grow after Frances was born, providing the wealth that made many opportunities available to her. Because Therese Adler was wounded by the loss of her first-born son, Murry, at age four, she lavished attention on her surviving children. She imparted to David and Frances a deep appreciation of fine art and music, insisting they become fluent in German (which was spoken at home) and French.

The pampered young Frances, described by one of her grandsons as "definitely a princess," grew up on Prospect Avenue in Gilded Age splendor in one of the magnificent houses that defined the neighborhood, whose styles ran the gamut of Victorian and Edwardian architecture.

While Therese encouraged Frances's cultural education, her formal education ended when she graduated from high school, and it was expected that she should marry into a wealthy East Coast family. But the three-year European tour with brother David ingrained in Frances's psyche a love of the avant-garde. During that time, she met some of the greatest artisans in the field—Jean-Michel Frank and Alberto Giacometti, in particular—and she would become a champion of their work, incorporating their designs in nearly all of her commissions. She had had ambition to be a concert pianist, but when that didn't work out, she turned her well-traveled eye to interior design. In 1916, she married polo player Felton Broomall Elkins, and it was her renovation of Casa Amesti (with David Adler) that started Frances's path to a career in decorating. •

<hr>

OPPOSITE David Adler and Fannie on the banks of Lake Michigan, circa 1907.

ABOVE LEFT TO RIGHT Fannie Adler on the Promenade des Anglais, Nice, circa 1915. The Charles A. Stonehill house in Glencoe, Illinois, David Adler's first commission, circa 1961, just before its demolition.

THE 1920s

The dawn of the 1920s saw Frances Elkins eight months pregnant and immersed with her brother, David Adler, in the restoration of Casa Amesti, the 1834 Monterey colonial-style Spanish adobe that would soon become the first expression of the Elkins style.

OPPOSITE Detail of The Jardins de Palais Royal,
a circa-1805 French scenic wallpaper,
reprinted and expanded in 1924 by Charles Huard,
in the upstairs hall at Casa Amesti.

ABOVE Felton and Frances Elkins's San Francisco apartment, around 1921, as decorated by Frances.

OPPOSITE CLOCKWISE FROM TOP LEFT Receipt for an identity card Frances presented to the Paris mayor's office, 1926. Frances's mother, Therese Adler, and Frances's daughter, Katherine Elkins, and terrier in Nice, winter 1926. The cover of a Dollar Steamship Lines brochure, early 1920s. Frances spent the winter of 1922–1923 visiting China and Japan. A Biarritz travel poster. Frances rented a Biarritz villa in the mid- to late-1920s, where her luncheons and dinners included the "leaders of French society" according to a 1927 San Francisco Chronicle item. Painting of the Grand Canal, Venice, circa 1740 by Canaletto. The first known newspaper mention of Frances taking "a house for the summer" in Italy was in 1928. Place Vendôme, Paris, sometime around 1926. Frances often stayed at the Hôtel Ritz (right) and was known to have shopped at the Coty store (left).

THE COUPLE WERE CARRYING on their active social life centered on parties, cultural events, polo, and golf among the elite of San Francisco, the Monterey Peninsula, and Southern California from their home in Hillsborough, just south of San Francisco, and from an apartment in the city.

Her creative work throughout the decade ahead would propel Frances from being a gregarious San Francisco high-society matron noted for her smart wardrobe and her marriage to a dashing millionaire polo-playing club-man to a nationally known interior designer. By the early 1930s, she would be recognized by her peers as one of the front-runners in her profession. New York decorator Sister Parish (1910–1994), who began her career in 1933, told the *San Francisco Chronicle* in a 1981 interview about the two ladies who commanded the decorating profession at the time she entered it: "When I started, no one was working. There was Elsie de Wolfe, and there was Mrs. Elkins (California decorator Frances Elkins) out here, and that was about all. Women stayed at home."[2] *House Beautiful* would give Frances her first major media

recognition in its illustrated article on Casa Amesti in December 1924.

By the 1920s, Frances's extensive early cultural exposure—as well as brother David's meticulous mentorship—would coalesce into what would become her mature decorating style. But in Frances's case, it was not just the exposure to the best architecture, decorative arts, and gardens in Europe, the United States, China, and Japan, but her ability to make meticulous observations of what she saw and express it in her decorating. In addition, the advantages provided by great family wealth had allowed her to witness firsthand the best of both traditional and contemporary painting, sculpture, music and dance, fashion, and domestic environments emerging in the exciting early years of the 20th century. This capacity to translate what she saw into beautiful, livable spaces certainly gave Frances a distinct advantage over other "lady decorators" of the 1920s.

Frances's style in the 1920s could be summarized as "a fresh slant on the traditional" as her rooms of the era captured the simplified essence of French provincial, Colonial/ Early American, English country, Spanish/Mexican, with hints of the emerging Art Deco, including floor treatments in projects she devised with David Adler. A unifying thread of her 1920s interiors, in addition to their use of high-quality of furnishings, textiles and finishes, was her ability to achieve clarity with scale and proportion, color and texture. Thus, her schemes stood out from many interiors designed for the wealthy in the 1920s which often had the static look of period rooms. As an innovator, Frances avoided stiff ornateness or ostentation, but could still use pattern on pattern, as well as many decorative objects in a single composition, without making a room look cluttered or fussy. What can also be seen clearly in her 1920s rooms was the sense of comfort and how the furnishings were scaled to happily accommodate men and women. This was a time when there was an unprecedented interest in quality traditional furnishings and the decorative arts across a wide spectrum of readers. The better shelter and society magazines of the time gave their audience a very deep, even intellectual, understanding of French, English, American and Asian antiques and art.

It is quite possible Frances had been unofficially working with Adler on decorating country houses, before she moved west and renovated Casa Amesti, according to a 1954 *San Francisco Chronicle* story about a museum-sponsored Elkins tribute tour: "Mrs. Elkins, famed in this country and in Europe as an interior designer, first started decorating homes in New York and Chicago designed by her brother, David Adler, a distinguished architect. When she came to California and settled in Monterey, she began working independently."

Few people enjoyed the success Frances achieved in her first—and arguably one of her most important—interior design project. At 31 years old, she found her secret garden in an adobe California house begun in 1834 and which, by 1850, had evolved into a pristine example of the Monterey colonial style, with second-floor balconies in front and back. The home was built by José Gallo Amesti (1788–1855), a Spanish Basque who arrived in Monterey under Mexican rule in 1822. Unusually, Casa Amesti remained in possession of the Amesti family until 1903; it was later jointly owned by a husband of one of the Amesti descendants who could not afford to retain it.

Felton Elkins bought the house for about $5,000 in May 1919, with the notion that once rehabilitated it would become their summer home. The high-profile couple—Felton noted for his polo-playing and amateur playwriting,

his new wife, Frances, admired for her beauty, captivating personality, and sense of fashion—were moving about seasonally among the social elite in San Francisco, Del Monte, and Santa Barbara from their base in Hillsborough.

In taking on the remodeling of Casa Amesti, Frances was not only at the vanguard in restoring an old California adobe for modern living but was perfectly positioned to take advantage of the postwar building boom in nearby Pebble Beach, which began around 1919. Members of her new West Coast circle—some based in San Francisco, but who would soon own second homes on the Monterey Peninsula, and others who would become year-round Pebble Beach residents—were some of Frances's first West Coast decorating clients.

Frances enlisted her brother, David Adler, to retrofit Casa Amesti. Like Frances, David had a strong respect for the architecture of the past and would undoubtedly realize that a period house with such good bones was well worth reviving. David maintained the look of the exterior, including the doors, windows, and window frames, as well as the essential interior structure. It cannot be overemphasized how impressed her friends were once they saw the Adler siblings' transformation of Casa Amesti and, in particular, the special flair Frances brought to the decoration.

Writing about Casa Amesti in her 1988 *Interior Design* feature on Frances Elkins, Lois Wagner Green observed

that Frances "determined, for her adobe house, to exploit the inherent, and hone the picturesque into the urbane, shaping a sophisticated break-away in décor." It stands to reason that only someone like Frances, with the soul of an artist and a deep love of antiquity, would have seen the potential in restoring a dilapidated home that lacked indoor plumbing, central heating, and an interior staircase.

By the time the house was first published in *House Beautiful* in 1924, Frances had created not only one of the most important landmarks of 20th-century interior design but an expression of a new approach to decoration that informed her sensibility and that of her clients for the rest of her life. (Frances appreciated the importance of Casa Amesti, willing it to the National Trust upon her death in 1953.)

A 1945 *House & Garden* feature on Casa Amesti noted that Frances "has given its interior a cosmopolitan elegance, predominantly Gallic, yet indebted to China, England and Italy for its individual flavor. She has a flair for achieving atmosphere from color: classic repose in the late afternoon grays and blues of an upstairs hall; a China silk brilliance in the vivid yellows and lapis lazuli of the big living room. . . . Her deft way with color is echoed in her confident blending of periods: French, English, Spanish, Italian, Chinese tapestries, an English horse painting by Sartorius and Venetian prints hang on the living room walls."

Frances "was able to use traditional furnishings in a fresh way. She had a special sense of scale and proportion, and a distinctive way of using color," said Diane Bower, longtime Casa Amesti docent, in a 1998 *Monterey Herald* feature on the house by Sedona Callahan. Frances had impressed upon this quietly imposing Mexican colonial building a style that was as refined as could be found anywhere in the great cities of the world.

Frances was now well on her way. •

<hr>

OPPOSITE LEFT David Adler photo by Eugene Hutchinson published in *Town & Country* in 1925. A Hutchinson portrait of Adler's wife, Katherine Keith Adler, appeared in the magazine the following year.

OPPOSITE RIGHT An undated photo of David Adler's office at Orchestra Hall, Chicago. The Art Institute, across the street, is visible through the window.

ABOVE LEFT An artist's rendering from a 1956 newspaper photo of the early 1920s dining room in the Jesse Strauss house, Frances and David's first official collaboration.

ABOVE RIGHT Frances with daughter, Katherine, Eugene Hutchinson portrait, circa 1925.

Frances Elkins

CASA AMESTI

MONTEREY, CALIFORNIA

1920–1953

CASA AMESTI WAS A prime example of the Monterey colonial style, with its balconies on the second floor and what *California Arts & Architecture* called in 1932 "an architecture of most graceful proportions and subtle charm and having withal a great dignity." Frances also saw the beauty of the place and along with her husband, Felton, purchased Casa Amesti for $5,000. It would become a landmark moment in her decorating career.

Frances enlisted her brother, David Adler, to retrofit it, knowing he would respect the house's history and original architecture. Adler kept the exterior look, but the addition of fluted door surrounds, an English mantelpiece in the living room, or sala, dentil cornices, and other classical details gave it a slightly more formal mood, without inhibiting its original humble simplicity. Frances and David were able to reclaim most of the redwood floors and planked ceiling, while adding closets, bathrooms, and other modern conveniences that reduced the size of certain rooms but enhanced their livability.

Frances created well-modulated spaces throughout with fine European and American antiques, a few pieces of new furniture, and a masterful use of color in furnishings and decorative objects. Jean-Michel Frank's minimalist plaster table lamps, ceiling fixtures, and sconces were also part of the mix. The use of strong colors against white walls was a fearless proclamation for her time.

Frances had hoped that with her interior decoration, Casa Amesti would become a museum open to the public, leaving it to the National Trust for Historical Preservation in her will. The Old Capital Club, a private membership men's social organization, has leased the house from the Trust since the late 1950s. Over the years, the club has made efforts to preserve some of the rooms decorated by Frances and to allow public tours. •

RIGHT The living room, or sala, was the most celebrated room in the house. A 1932 photo shows several conversation groups symmetrically placed around an antique English partner's desk.

ABOVE A rare circa 1950 Tony Duquette color image toward the dining room doors shows the sala in its original splendor, with all the vibrant fabrics and rugs chosen by Frances and used in her lifetime. Most of these more luxurious textiles no longer survive.

OPPOSITE TOP A 1945 photo for *House & Garden,* with a view of the opposite side of the room.

OPPOSITE BOTTOM FROM LEFT The exterior of Casa Amesti in a 1969 photo, with the French stone dogs Frances placed on either side of the front door. A portrait of Frances by her friend Eugenia (Gene) McComas, between 1920 and 1924.

PREVIOUS LEFT A 1934 photo of the red-tiled entry hall draws the eye toward a lovely vista of the rear garden. The colonial-style wall sconces were probably made by Edward F. Caldwell & Co., which supplied innumerable light fixtures to Frances throughout her career.

PREVIOUS RIGHT, CLOCKWISE FROM TOP LEFT The upstairs hallway with its vivid blue-and-white hand-blocked Palais Royal Zuber wallpaper. "For the library . . . Elkins bought carved blue bookcases, touched with gold, from the south of France," explained *House & Garden* in 1948. Paneling in the window well was painted to match the antique boiserie. Bookbindings in reds, browns, blues, and greens complement the bookshelves. The Adler-designed solarium in 1950. Adler made the windows so that each pane of glass is set into embrasures rather than using large panes of glass with the mullions applied over the glass.

ABOVE The dining room as it appeared in 1934. The room was notable for its pale-cream palette from the painted furniture accented by browns and golds. Such a neutral background would allow Frances, as hostess nonpareil, to create endless tablescapes using her enormous collection of colorful table linens and dinnerware. She entertained constantly at Casa Amesti, particularly with small luncheons or dinners, when she was not traveling. Her annual New Year's Eve parties were the most coveted invitation on the Monterey Peninsula.

OPPOSITE Fred Lyon's 1983 photo of the dining room shows Frances's final curtain treatment of fringed gold-silk curtains and lambrequins. For this image, daughter Katherine Elkins Boyd arranged the table with her mother's china, linens, and Misia Sert coral decorations.

PREVIOUS, LEFT David Adler's bedroom—with its bird's-eye maple four-poster bed covered in an 18th-century crewelwork bedspread—in a 1934 photo from *Country Life in America*.

PREVIOUS, RIGHT Top: A 1983 photo of the dressing alcove shows a Louis XVI giltwood mirror, dressing table articles including brushes and mirrors, and two sets of small table lamps. Bottom: The wallpaper in the alcove is Place Vendôme. A pristine remnant of the paper (bottom) shows the pattern and true colors as they would have appeared on the walls in the 1930s.

ABOVE AND OPPOSITE TOP The two guest rooms off the downstairs hall, both done in red and white, mixed with the warm tones of French provincial furniture selected by Frances in Europe. In one room, a four-poster canopy bed, curtains, chaise, and side chair are covered in a bold red-and-ecru 18th-century toile de Nantes. In the other, an old red-and-white toile de Jouy in a delicate pattern is quilted to cover twin beds.

OPPOSITE BOTTOM Samples of the red toile believed to have been used on bed hangings in the bedroom above are held by the Elkins archives at Monterey Peninsula College.

ABOVE A painting of Frances's bedroom by legendary interior designer Mark Hampton shows a fitted shell-pink bedspread with a folded white-fur throw trimmed in shell pink. He had seen the room in a 1945 *House & Garden* photo. For his 1992 book *Legendary Decorators of the Twentieth Century*, Hampton would paint the bedroom in color, using the magazine image as reference. He declared that "In spite of all its old-fashioned elements, it was still a room of clean, uncluttered modernity."

OPPOSITE An unpublished photo of the room, circa 1930. Around that time, Frances had given the room a makeover, likely influenced by the spare modernist ethos of her French designer friend Jean-Michel Frank. The white-on-white rooms were likely influenced by English decorator Syrie Maugham. The white four-poster bed has a white hobnail bedspread and the same fur throw as seen in Hampton's painting. The white fishnet canopy was trimmed with a sturdy ball fringe, with the large tassels on the four posts made of the same size fringe.

The Larkin House

MONTEREY, CALIFORNIA · 1923

LIKE FRANCES ELKINS, Alice Larkin Toulmin became enchanted by a mid-19th-century Monterey adobe. The house in question was a family home built in 1834 by Alice's grandfather Thomas Oliver Larkin. The elder Larkin was a prosperous Monterey businessman and the sole U.S. consul to Alta California in the Mexican era before statehood. The New Hampshire–born Alice did not visit her grandfather's house until she was forty-three years old, having bought it sight unseen. Alice had become smitten with the idea of owning it and bringing back much of its original furniture, which she had inherited.

Alice and her English husband, Harry W. Toulmin, moved to Monterey in 1922 and became Frances's neighbors when they bought the historic adobe for $10,000.

Known as the Larkin House, the residence is now one of the treasures of the California State Parks system. With its overhanging eaves and second-story veranda, the house is considered the most perfect (and the first) example of the often-mimicked Monterey style.

Thomas Larkin had wanted to construct a house in the typical New England style of his native Massachusetts, but with a scarcity of local redwood, he instead fitted out the walls in whitewashed adobe.

Frances assisted Alice in refurbishing the adobe without changing its layout or interior architecture. In addition to the inherited furniture, Alice also owned antiques and ornaments purchased during her many overseas jaunts. Alice wanted the decorator to give the house the same crisp, edited quality and careful use of color as Frances's newly invigorated Casa Amesti.

Frances came up with the subtle paint palette for the rooms. "Soft but clear solid background colors predominate, . . . rose, lavender, apricot and pale blue give the . . . a slightly old-fashioned (but certainly not musty) atmosphere," wrote Martin Filler in a 1983 *House & Garden*.

Filler also noted that Frances's simple arrangements made the rooms look modern for the early 1920s and, indeed, timeless. Frances realized that Monterey adobes,

with their whitewashed walls, were well disposed to set off nice things.

Frances also helped Alice choose the textiles for the upholstered furniture and curtains, further enlivening the house. Filler also wrote that Alice's and Frances's "passion" gave it a "humanity" lacking in many historic houses.

Alice donated Larkin House to the State of California in 1957, with all of its antiques, rugs, and objets d'art in situ; it is the most intact residence Frances ever had a hand in decorating. •

ABOVE An early postcard of the house.

OPPOSITE TOP In the parlor, English antiques and furniture pretty much as first arranged in the 1920s. A painting of Alice's grandmother, Rachel Hobson Holmes Larkin, hangs above the mantel.

OPPOSITE BOTTOM LEFT Alice's bedroom, featuring the imposing Chinese opium bed she purchased in 1920. Alongside is a teakwood table bought in Thailand on the same trip.

OPPOSITE BOTTOM RIGHT In the Rose Guest Bedroom, a provincial commode, an Empire trumeau mirror, and a rush-seated chair, all French, complement painted and gilded antique mirrors and a Chinese rug. The pale-peach chintz on the bed hangings is also used for the curtains.

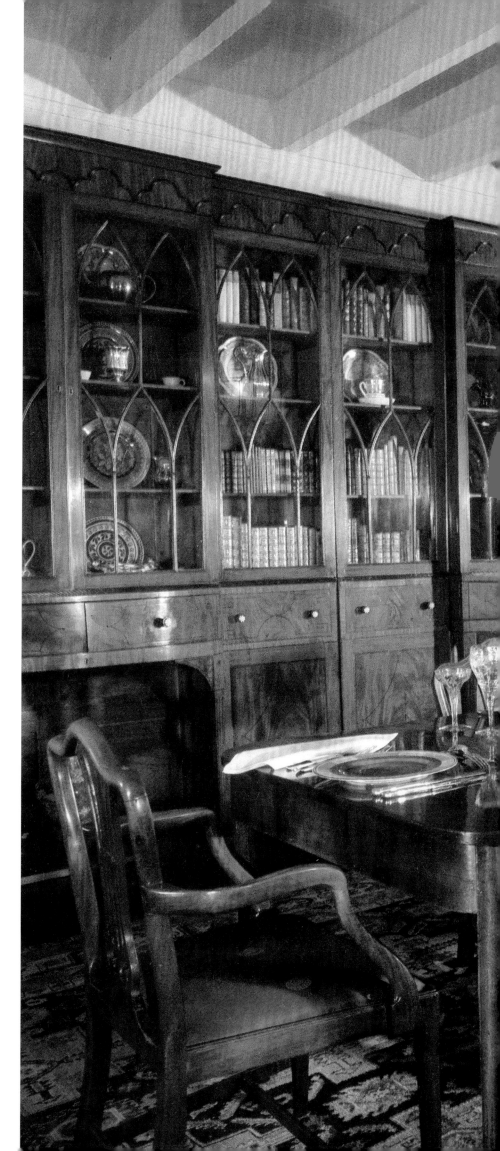

RIGHT As shown in 1983, the low-ceilinged dining room with exposed beams is commanded by a Hepplewhite Gothic transitional-style breakfront, circa 1795, purchased by the Toulmins in Ireland. Late-18th-century English table and chairs: the chair seats were covered in a Scalamandré reproduction of the cobalt-blue Chinese-tribute silk selected in the 1920s. The room is lit by Moroccan lanterns Frances used in many other projects. A Persian mahal rug, which Frances is believed to have chosen in the 1940s to replace the room's first oriental rugs, covers the redwood floor. Also seen is some of Alice's 1920s Wedgwood china.

Mrs. Carolyn Morse Ely

LAKE BLUFF, ILLINOIS · 1925

HEIRESS TO A STEEL AND ORE fortune, Mrs. Carolyn Morse Ely first commissioned David Adler in 1914 to design a house in Lake Bluff, Illinois. Two gatehouses were built by 1916, but completion was delayed until the early 1920s because of the First World War.

Adler's inspiration for the French country-style house, clad in brick painted a soft yellow, was the Pavillon de La Lanterne, a hunting lodge on the grounds of Versailles. Like its French counterpart, the house was steeped in sunlight, with card room, living room, hall, and dining room creating an enfilade.

It is thought that Frances, Adler's sister, furnished the house. Surviving correspondence between Ely and Frances from 1929 to 1936 about Ely's 1930 Chicago apartment indicate they had been longtime friends and that Ely deferred to Frances in all matters of decoration. When Ely sold the house in 1928, Frances would later repurpose much of the furniture for the Chicago apartment.

Augusta Owen Patterson's description of house's exterior in a 1925 *Town & Country* seems equally applicable to the interiors: "The composition holds perfectly together, the story is told elegantly and without elaboration. The result is charm and a delicious flavor of France." •

OPPOSITE The warm golden-brown of the living room's Louis XV boiserie make an engaging background for simple furniture in scale with the dimensions of the room. "The pine, is of course, unstained and unwaxed, giving full value to the natural color," wrote Patterson in *Town & Country*. Patterson praised the "unobtrusive but artistically important mantel." A clean-lined modern upholstered chair keeps company with a Louis XV settee. Pagoda-roofed decorations at the fireplace, an English mahogany Chinese Chippendale end table and a multicolored Chinese rug add Oriental notes. The simple planked floor gives the room an unpretentious ambience.

ABOVE A 1925 photo of the west (garden) elevation shows a pleasing balance between rectangular main house and the north and south wings at either end.

ABOVE At one end of the living room, furniture is perfectly balanced between two doors, one of which leads to the North Porch. On the wall is a mid-18th-century Chinese export polychrome wallpaper panel depicting equestrian figures at various pursuits amid pavilions and mountainous landscapes. Circa 1720 Regency caned fauteuils flank a tuxedo sofa. Chinese vases converted into table lamps sit on unmatched end tables. Simple curtains, likely in a solid-colored linen, provide an element of modernity. The lamps, fauteuils, and panel would later reemerge in Mrs. Ely's Chicago living room.

OPPOSITE, TOP "An excellent example of the use of patterned wall-paper and matching fabrics . . . which transfers us to the atmosphere of France," wrote Nancy McClelland about the guest room in a 1927 issue of *The Delineator*. The toile de Jouy, Le Ballon de Gonesse, used throughout was designed by Jean-Baptiste Huet for Oberkampf & Cie and depicts the first hot-air balloon flight.

Circa 1790 French Directoire painted daybeds with pediments and open columns are mixed with a provincial walnut fauteuil and Italian neoclassical painted side chair, both late 19th century.

OPPOSITE, BOTTOM LEFT The brick walls of the North Porch are painted a darker color from the white-painted South Porch (not shown), setting off what are likely Elkins's typical use of fresh colors and patterns here. The glazed herringbone floor, potted plants, ethnic rugs, floral pillows, and distinctive wicker chair and chaise, possibly from English firm G.W. Scott, contribute to the relaxed atmosphere. Frances often paired painted French-style rush-seated chairs and French-inspired tables to keep rooms from being overly formal. The paneled door offers a glimpse into the card room.

OPPOSITE, BOTTOM RIGHT Detail of the guest room toile in blue.

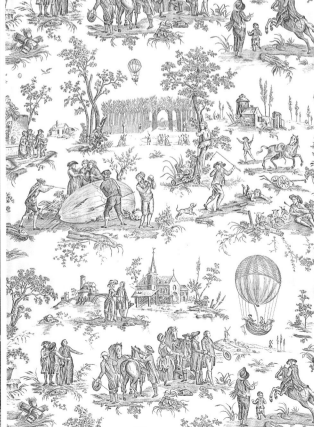

Shoreacres Country Club

LAKE BLUFF, ILLINOIS · 1924

FRANCES STARTED WORK on the Shoreacres Country Club, likely her first public commission, in 1924 and possibly continuing into the 1940s. Designed by her brother, David Adler, the white colonial-style clapboard building had green shutters and window boxes filled seasonally with red geraniums. Adler used the forms of early-American farmhouses as inspiration.

"The interiors have that demure and clean cheerfulness which is possible to the Colonial motive," wrote Augusta Owen Patterson in *Town & Country* in 1925. Frances would design other similar schemes inspired by the colonial style, including a guest bedroom in the Charles Goodspeed apartment in Chicago and several rooms in the William McCormick Blair house in Lake Bluff.

Chicago upholsterer William J. Quigley and Company supplied some of the furnishings, chintz fabrics, red willow wallpaper, and antique pewter; Stanley Field, a residential client of David Adler's and a Shoreacres club member, helped secure some of the clubhouse's antiques.

Frances's signature style of contrasting colors and textures figured greatly at Shoreacres. Patterson noted how in the living room, "Quite unexpectedly, in view of the color foundation of green, the long couch before the fireplace and certain of the chairs are upholstered in red leather." An overstuffed lounge chair and a small sofa were covered in quilted Hollyhock fabric. The fabric was obviously a favorite, as Frances also used it in the living room of the 1926 William McCormick Blair house and in a sitting room in the Richard Crane house in 1928. Hollyhock was also chosen for the glazed cotton curtains.

The rooms were decorated in a very pale green, setting off the vivid scenic Décor Chinois wallpaper by Jean Zuber, first made in 1832. At the time, the paper was mistakenly identified as antique Chinese wallpaper. In the early 1920s, Adler is known to have visited Beauport, the Massachusetts summer home of interior designer Henry Davis Sleeper, and Frances may have toured the home with him as well. Beauport's Belfry Bedroom featured Décor Chinois paired

with a pale-green paint trim, a combination that could easily have inspired the Shoreacres living room with its green woodwork.

As is often said of her work, Frances preferred that most of her public commissions have the inviting comfort of a well-appointed residence. "TO ALL INTENTS A PRIVATE HOME" is how *The Spur* described the living room in 1930. "The Colonial feeling in the lounge of Shoreacres is finely preserved, with any semblance of a 'clubroom' conspicuous by its absence." ·

OPPOSITE The hallway was paneled in pine, as shown in this 1920s photo. Augusta Owen Patterson called out the "arched panels with the crossed stiles in the lower part of the wainscot," which could have been modeled after a period room at the Metropolitan Museum of Art. Simple antique chairs against the wall do not impede the traffic flow. The black floor anchors all the pine.

ABOVE A 1920s view of the main entrance.

LEFT Columns and arches divided the main living area into north and south lounges. Shown here is a 1920s view of the south living room. A large broken pediment at the top of a carved frame encases a painting of sailing ships above the fireplace.

ABOVE A detail of the colorful Décor Chinois Zuber wallpaper used throughout.

Mr. & Mrs. Albert D. Lasker

LAKE FOREST, ILLINOIS · 1926–1936)

ONE OF FRANCES'S MOST prodigious undertakings was Mill Road Farm, the whitewashed brick country house of advertising legend Albert D. Lasker and wife, Flora. David Adler designed the 55-room main residence and completed it in 1926, taking inspiration from the mansarded manor houses of 18th-century France. The residence was only one of the many structures on the estate, which covered nearly 500 acres, that the siblings worked on together. In addition to the extensive rooms of the main house, Frances fitted out the property's two pool houses and a recreation center with a private movie theater. And it is believed Frances also assisted Flora Lasker with furnishing the guesthouse. The expansive grounds contained a working farm, flower gardens, tennis courts, stables, a garage, and a private 18-hole golf course.

The Lasker estate was designed for the family's extravagant summer entertaining; the rest of the year, the couple and their three children lived in a Chicago apartment. Frances and David worked on the interiors from about 1926 until Flora's death in 1936. Lasker donated the estate to the University of Chicago in 1939, after which the main house was sold to private owners and the rest subdivided into residential parcels.

The Lasker commission gave Frances free reign—and an almost unlimited budget—to create memorable rooms with her traditional Gallic flavor, She had numerous pieces of furniture shipped directly from France, including a pair of bombé commodes and Louis XV- and XVI–style chairs. These French touches were eclectically paired with vibrant Chinese rugs and blue-and-white floral chintz on the chairs, love seat, and sofa. The scale of the rooms Frances was tasked to decorate was impressive. For example, the English regency table and chairs in the dining room, acquired in Europe, could seat up to 20 people. In her 1933 feature for *Town & Country*, Augusta Owen Patterson praised Frances's interiors, writing that they had "the advantage of some of the finest provincial French furniture in America, used with a very fresh point of view and a graceful color design." •

OPPOSITE In 1939 called the Lasker powder room an "elegant French provincial dressing room painted light gray with pale silk curtains. The furniture is covered in old blue silk." Closets were set into each of the corners. The opulent French birdcage chandelier is most likely from Maison Baguès in Paris.

ABOVE A 1967 view of the forecourt shows the main block of the house with its gray window shutters. In the foreground, a pool with a cherub fountain.

LEFT The majestic salon in 1941 had painted Louis XV pine paneled walls and antique oak parquet de Versailles floors. The wedding cake crystal chandelier is from Baguès circa 1910–20. Portrait of Flora Lasker hangs at the far end. Brown-leather bergères, blue-linen upholstered fauteuils, and a rare Chinese rug show Frances's flair for mixing furnishings.

FOLLOWING LEFT The oval-domed library was painted canary yellow and includes Jean-Michel Frank's plaster table lamps and a modern coffee table (possibly by Frank). Faux-leather bindings covered some of the doors. The 1941 photo is the only known color record of the dining room. Panels of wallpaper feature the Greek muses in medallions depicting the six arts, along a border of neoclassical columns. A carving of Louis XIV hangs above the blue marble fireplace.

FOLLOWING RIGHT The bedroom walls were French paneling of bleached oak. Frances deftly mixed styles: modern white stick lamps, a pewter pitcher, Chinese painted plates, a Louis XV marble-top commode. The guest room was in a contemporary style with twin beds by Paul Rodocanachi for Jean-Michel Frank. (Whether Rodocanachi originals or Frances's approved adaptations is unknown.) A neoclassical chair is set before the kneehole desk with double-armed girandole lamps.

Colonel & Mrs. Allen Griffin

PEBBLE BEACH, CALIFORNIA · 1926–1935

ONE OF FRANCES'S EARLY residential commissions in Pebble Beach was the 1926 home of Hester Griffin, then Mrs. Arthur Hately. Work came easily after Frances completed the widely praised transformation of Casa Amesti, her Monterey home, in 1920. The Hatelys had stayed at the Larkin house when they first moved to the Monterey Peninsula in 1922, and Hester became an admirer of Frances's work after visiting the nearby Casa Amesti. Hester purchased a secluded property on the 17 Mile Drive on which to build her dream home and hired Santa Barbara architect George Washington Smith to design the residence and Frances to decorate it. The estate was called Cheviot Hill because of the sheep that grazed nearby.

For Cheviot Hill, Frances bought a great deal of furniture on an initial buying trip to France, and Hester would join her in Paris to buy more furniture for the living room. The decoration of the home continued into the mid-1930s. In 1935, Hester remarried to Colonel Allen Griffin, publisher of the *Monterey Peninsula Herald* newspaper. Hester and Allen would become two of Frances's closest friends. When Colonel Griffin was sent to China on a diplomatic mission in 1949, Frances instructed Hester on what Asian antiques, pottery, and ceramics he should purchase, and these new acquisitions became part of the mix.

The twenty-four-room home was designed by Smith in his signature Spanish Colonial Revival style, with a tile roof and a second-story balcony as a nod to the Monterey regional substyle. Smith was one of the many great architects with which Frances collaborated. They also worked together on the Cypress Point clubhouse around 1930. •

LEFT A 1940s exterior view shows a Mediterranean-inspired garden with a patio fountain.

OPPOSITE For the entryway staircase, Frances mixed a black-and-white Moroccan runner with blue marbleized Venetian paper wainscoting. The red-tiled entry with a 17th-century oak chair is reminiscent of the downstairs hall at Casa Amesti. A bold Afghani rug adds a vigorous note of red and blue.

RIGHT The living room fireplace seating in 1983, with the only update to the original scheme being the chairs, designed by Frances, now reupholstered in a peachy corduroy by Michael Taylor, who also had two more fabricated. Artist Margaret Bruton designed the square terrazzo-top coffee table. Eric Haupt's painting of Arthur Hately Jr. hangs above the fireplace.

BELOW The living room in 1952, with all of Frances's original decor. Colonel and Mrs. Griffin are shown hosting painter Elizabeth Johnstone Duquette, wife of artist Tony Duquette, who took the two slides.

OPPOSITE Frances perfected an environment of understated graciousness by contrasting periods and textures.

RIGHT The dining room, seen here in 1983, was formal yet unpretentious. Frances covered the walls with a playful antique hand-painted French mural on canvas, circa 1820, depicting early methods of transportation. The 18th-century English three-pedestal table with English Georgian mahogany chairs with polished blue-leather seats once belonged to Hester's parents. White Ming chargers and a collection of heirloom silver grace the Sheraton serpentine-front sideboard. A blue handwoven Portuguese rug covers the doweled hardwood floor. Picasso porcelain vases and Mexican Talavera pottery sit in the window well.

Hotel Del Monte

MONTEREY, CALIFORNIA · 1926

ONE OF FRANCES'S EARLY PUBLIC commissions was decorating the guest rooms, cafes, and lounges of the rebuilt Hotel Del Monte, which had been severely damaged by fire in 1924. The capacious hotel was less than two miles from Casa Amesti. From 1880 on the Hotel Del Monte was one of the finest luxury hotels in the country, drawing eminent guests from around the world. Its amenities included tennis courts and pools, as well as a racetrack, polo field, and golf course. Frances and her husband, Felton, had spent the first month of their summer 1918 honeymoon at the hotel, and she would attend many dinners and special events there.

The 1926 special issue of *Keeler's Hotel Weekly* reported that "the bedrooms are furnished in the Spanish style, . . . a bright, colorful effect being maintained, pleasing to the eyes and exceedingly comfortable." *Keeler's* also noted that "the Basque period in Spanish decoration was used in the bedrooms." Frances had spent much time in Biarritz, in Basque country, buying fabrics to bring back to the U.S.

In 1927, the *Los Angeles Times* society column described Frances's decoration for the Golf Grill as "chic," writing that it had become "a favorite spot for tea, not only among the active athletes who pause to refresh themselves after their eighteen holes but among the more leisurely observers as well." •

RIGHT Frances and Relda Morse on the hotel's polo field, 1929. Samuel F.B. Morse, Relda's husband, was president of the Del Monte Properties Company, which purchased the hotel in 1919. A 1927 cover for *Game & Gossip*, a magazine created by Morse to publicize the social and sporting activities of the "smart set" on the Monterey Peninsula.

OPPOSITE Examples of three guest rooms decorated by Frances, which show her commitment to comfort and convenience. The rooms have a crisply tailored quality. She often chose chenille or candlewick spreads for her hotel commissions, and many of the rooms had tole hanging lights or ceiling lamps with colored paper shades that harmonized with the decor.

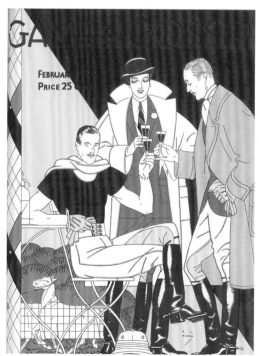

Casa Blanca

THE STEVENSON HOUSE

MONTEREY, CALIFORNIA · 1927–1947

FROM 1927 TO 1947, THE HISTORIC Robert Louis Stevenson House in downtown Monterey was Frances's professional headquarters—the nerve center from which she executed many of her most celebrated designs. Stevenson House was one of Monterey's most famous adobes, so Frances's decision to use it for her business shows her keen appreciation of the past and the romantic appeal old architecture held for her.

Originally Madame Girardin's French Hotel, the building was renowned because a then-unknown Scottish writer named Robert Louis Stevenson spent three months there in 1879. Stevenson wrote to a friend about the "splendid" and "airy" upstairs rooms. Shortly after the writer's death in 1894—world famous by then as the author of *Treasure Island* and *The Strange Case of Dr. Jekyll and Mr. Hyde*—the building was renamed in his honor.

By the 1920s, Stevenson house had become home to several artists. In 1926, however, the building was threatened with demolition. Francis McComas, an artist friend of Frances's, saw the need to save Stevenson House and persuaded two of his patrons to buy it. In moving her business there in 1927, Frances brought some of the artists with studios in the building into her fold: August Gay made picture frames and paneling; his wife, Marcelle Chaix, sewed curtains. The three Bruton sisters, including Margaret Bruton, made mosaic-covered tables.

Offices and showrooms were downstairs, and workshops were on the second floor. By the 1930s, Frances would employ sixty people including furniture makers, upholsterers, and seamstresses. Her business continued to thrive during the Great Depression, so Frances was able to keep many local artists and craftspeople employed.

Frances used the atmospheric Stevenson House as a gallery. Shoppers could wander into the building and peruse furniture for sale. •

OPPOSITE TOP AND BOTTOM Frances was one of the first American decorators to use French provincial furniture, and it was featured prominently in the gallery at Stevenson House.

ABOVE Frances in one of a series of formal portraits taken around 1940. What may be a Matisse painting is visible behind her.

LEFT An ad that ran in a 1929 issue of *Game & Gossip*. Frances initially called her business Casa Blanca (White House) because of the building's white-painted adobe exterior.

Mr. & Mrs. Charles Goodspeed

CHICAGO, ILLINOIS · 1927–1930

THE TWO-STORY PENTHOUSE of the Goodspeeds at 2430 North Lakeview Avenue was one of many elegant Chicago apartments with interior architecture by David Adler and decor by Frances Elkins. With styles ranging from Georgian to Art Deco to colonial, the unit crowned an eighteen-story co-op building built in 1926. Occupying over 5,500 square feet, the apartment had sweeping views of Lincoln Park and Lake Michigan.

Charles "Barney" Goodspeed was the son of an affluent Cleveland steel magnate. His wife, Elizabeth "Bobsy" Fuller Goodspeed, was the daughter of a Chicago doctor. Mrs. Goodspeed, known for her outgoing personality, beauty, and fashion flair, was president of the Arts Club of Chicago from 1931 to 1941. Her home was a conduit for bringing culture to Chicago: she hosted Gertrude Stein, George Gershwin, and Thornton Wilder, among other greats.

"Her interest in art filled her beautiful apartment with modern paintings," wrote *Chicago Tribune* columnist Thalia in 1950. The rooms were adorned with paintings by Picasso, Matisse, and Braque, and included some fine Art Deco furnishings such as a clean-lined pine and ebony cabinet by Ruhlmann.

The seamless collaboration between the siblings is evident in both the architectural and decorative details. For example, the Georgian carved mantel that features in the drawing room was purchased by Mrs. Goodspeed and Adler in England; its size required that the planned ceiling be raised by one foot to accommodate the pediment. Frances and David must have factored in the element of surprise when planning the dining room, where traditional most definitely merged with the spirit of Art Moderne. Ebonized maple floors are outlined in inlaid nickel in a guilloche, or braided, ribbon pattern. At the four corners, on a bias, a leaf pattern is set in the floor in nickel lozenges. The octagonal ceiling inset echoed the outlines of the floor pattern, with an acanthus-leaf border. The floor and ceiling were a counterpoint to the rectangular room. A crystal chandelier and wall sconces were the light sources in a room that intentionally

did not have electricity at the time and was illuminated by candlelight after dark. •

ABOVE A plump sofa with rounded back and rolled arms and a fringed winged chair define one of the seating groups in the living room. Syrie Maugham supplied the black lacquer chinoiserie tables as well as a pair of Queen Anne mirrors, one of which is seen here.

OPPOSITE The dining room's simple white Georgian fireplace with triangular pediment and white marble pilasters with capitals of nickel amplify the classical tones. The English Regency mahogany pedestal dining table is circa 1815, with English Regency mahogany Klismos-inspired chairs with saber legs.

ABOVE Mrs. Goodspeed in a white Vionnet hostess gown sits on a fringed oyster-white divan under her portrait by Bernard Boutet de Monvel. Two matching doorways can be seen on either side, but one is actually a set of false doors, exemplifying Adler's obsession with balance and symmetry. *Town & Country* observed: "It is a room of fine, calculated sobriety, founded on an intelligent comprehension of values."

LEFT The portrait of Mrs. Goodspeed shows her next to one of the chinoiserie tables in the drawing room.

OPPOSITE, TOP In this colonial-style guest room, a green botanical wallpaper, a pair of four-poster beds (likely antiques) with ball-fringed canopies, and candlewick bedspreads set the flavor.

OPPOSITE, BOTTOM Mrs. Goodspeed's sun-filled Directoire-style sitting room had cool-green marbleized walls and door surrounds and curtains in a copper-colored taffeta, with a frieze of stars and paterae on the cornice. In the niche is a photomural of a snapshot she had taken when visiting the Taj Mahal; a velvet-covered Empire daybed sits in front.

Mr. & Mrs. Robert Mandel

HIGHLAND PARK, ILLINOIS

1926–1935

THROUGHOUT THE LATE 1920s and into the 1930s, Frances decorated a Normandy-style chateau designed by David Adler for Robert Mandel and his wife, Stella (née Kaufman). Mandel was board chairman of the Mandel Brothers Department Store his family founded in Chicago in the mid-1850s. Fronting Lake Michigan, the limestone, brick, and half-timbered residence had a roof of orange Ludovici tile shingles. The design was influenced by French country houses Adler saw in his travels and in books of historic houses. Richard Pratt, author of *David Adler: The Architect and His Work* (1970), characterized it as "almost a story-book house."

Frances created appealing mixtures of furnishings throughout the house. Primarily French traditional in spirit, the interiors were embellished with Asian antiques and porcelains. Frances's eye for simplicity, creative juxtaposition, and modern comfort created an effect that transcended the time-dated atmosphere of period rooms.

Frances filled the house with fine antiques she purchased from numerous vendors in Paris, Versailles, Biarritz, London, Madrid, and the U.S. The vast selection of furnishings included rugs, lamps, and chandeliers from Syrie Maugham, and Chinese rugs and Tang figurines from Gump's of San Francisco. She also incorporated 17th-century parquet floors reclaimed from a French chateau.

In the mid-1930s, Frances also decorated Robert and Stella Mandel's Beverly Hills house, previously owned by Academy Award–winning actress Marie Dressler. •

RIGHT Old oak paneling from Europe establishes a rich ambience in the living room, or Music Room, circa 1930. Frances could successfully mix sophisticated furniture such as Louis XV chairs and a coromandel screen with a rustic desk. Two Louis XV fauteuils in a pale-beige fabric sit on a rug of zebra skin. A fanciful chandelier with scrolling foliated arms and cage complemented rocaille sconces at the Louis XVI-style marble fireplace. A French daybed in a yellow fabric sits under a 1928 portrait of Stella Mandel.

CLOCKWISE FROM TOP LEFT The library, in a 1935 stereo card, also the home's gallery, was fitted out in Bavarian pine purchased in Europe. More than 46 feet long, the room had an imported Louis XV fireplace and bookcases set into the boiserie. Folding leather chairs surround the square French provincial piece used as a game table, anchored on a zebra rug. Mozart and Beethoven busts are set on marble plinths. A bodhisattva statue on a marble stand in the rotunda, 1935. The solarium had a polished red-brick floor, white-brick walls, and dark beams and timbers accentuated with what is believed to have been mostly blue-and-white fabrics.

OPPOSITE TOP The dining room included a mix of French court and country furniture. A highlight was—and still is—a hand-painted antique chinoiserie wallpaper with birds, trees, and flowers in green, brown, and rose tones on a buff background.

OPPOSITE BOTTOM A late-1930s stereo view of Mrs. Mandel's dressing room (left). Its pale gray-green paneled walls—paired with lots of cream, white, and florals—exemplify Frances's mastery of simple color schemes to give a room of antiques a modern feeling. Frances used similar colors for Mr. Mandel's dressing room (right), with its cream-colored painted Louis XV boiserie with gold detailing.

Mr. & Mrs. Richard T. Crane, Jr.

IPSWICH, MASSACHUSETTS · 1927–1931

THE SUMMER HOME OF Richard T. Crane, Jr. and his wife, Florence, on the estate called Castle Hill was David Adler's largest residential commission, and certainly among his finest. The Chicago-based Mr. Crane was president of the Crane Co., which made plumbing fixtures and popularized the indoor bathroom. Adler had designed a winter home in 1916 for the Cranes in Jekyll Island, Georgia, and when the couple wanted a new house to replace their Italianate summer home at Castle Hill, they called Adler again. Adler's concept for the Cranes' new 59-room mansion, with its Stuart-style main facade, was based on 17th-century English Baroque houses like Eagle House and Belton House, the latter inspired by the work of Christopher Wren. The house, completed about 1927 and mostly decorated around 1928, was clad in small Holland brick and spectacularly sited above a sloping allée to the Atlantic Ocean, a half-mile away.

It had been assumed that Adler and Mrs. Crane had decorated the house. Frances's pre-1929 project files were discarded by her last assistant, Nelle Currie, after Frances's death. However, some recently discovered evidence sheds light on a probable collaboration: a 1929 letter from Frances to David in which she discusses china she wants David to buy for Mrs. Crane; a 1929 telegram from Mrs. Crane in Paris to Frances in Biarritz about silver doilies; a 1929 letter from David's office to Frances's office about furniture she wanted removed for the house; and, a 1931 Casa Blanca bank deposit slip noting funds paid by Mr. Crane. Newspaper accounts also confirm that Frances was in Europe from June to December in both 1927 and 1928, which would have coincided with the trips Adler was known to have made with the Cranes to hunt for furniture.

Architecture and cultural historian Michael Henry Adams, who has visited the home and reviewed period photos of the interiors, calls the living room "a perfect place for a cocktail party: the idea of sitting there and then the procession from the drawing room to the dining room and then to coffee in the library after dinner . . . " •

ABOVE An exterior view of the house.

OPPOSITE TOP TO BOTTOM The Georgian-paneled living room in circa-1935 photos by Mattie Edwards Hewitt shows an inviting mix of English period furniture enhanced with Chinese objects d'art and lacquer screens. A portrait by Joseph Wright of Derby hangs over the fireplace with inset mirrors.

OPPOSITE TOP AND BOTTOM The dining room (above) is the most fully restored room, with its original dining table, dining chairs with their ivory leather seats, and breakfast table recently donated by a Crane granddaughter. Curtains in a Tree of Life fabric are nearly identical to the original (below). The green damask wing chairs and green camelback sofa are close facsimiles to the originals, while the current rug evokes the cream and blue rug seen in Hewitt's photos.

ABOVE This guest bedroom, in a never-published photo, was one of two Chinoiserie-style rooms at Castle Hill. The bedroom exemplifies Frances's gift for layering different design elements.

THE
1930s

The 1930s were a momentous period in the career and the life of Frances Elkins, a time when she achieved many professional pinnacles.

AT A DEEPLY PERSONAL LEVEL, the decade began and ended with personal tragedies. First was the sudden death of her beloved sister-in-law Katherine Keith Adler in 1930[3], and the second was her mother's death in 1939.[4]

The 1930s would see the full flowering of what became known as the Frances Elkins style: the deft merging of the classical and the modern, always as aware of comfort as of style. During the decade, she would realize with David Adler some of their most superlative commissions, both country houses and city apartments. Frances was adding a new layer of sophistication not only from the spare elegance of Jean-Michel Frank, but from her many new sources from the world of the California decorative arts, including the brightly colored weavings of Dorothy Liebes.

David Adler is considered by many the finest American traditional country house architect of the 20th century. He was known for borrowing from and seamlessly combining many styles and periods. Frances was the interior designer on at least fifteen of Adler's fifty residential commissions. It has been said that she did her greatest work with Adler. Certainly, the rooms she decorated in Adler houses constitute many of her most memorable 1930s interiors.

David and Frances's common goal in the 1930s was creating large homes with exquisite detail and livability. The perfect proportions and graceful lines Adler insisted upon were exceptionally well suited to Frances's classical

modernist schemes. Her own unfailing sense of scale was always apparent in her many imaginative compositions.

Frances also began to integrate cutting edge Parisian decorative arts into a newly cohesive style, adding an additional twist to the traditional idiom she had perfected in the 1920s, with boldly original results. The French furniture

---

ABOVE LEFT Helen Potter Russell (at left) and Frances Elkins reviewing the pink china to be used in the Yerba Buena Club main dining room, November 1938.

ABOVE RIGHT Frances (far right) meeting actress Shirley Temple (center) on the 20th-Century Fox Studios lot, circa 1935. Also shown, from left: Irving Berlin, David Adler, Mrs. Ellin Berlin, and Mrs. Evelyn Marshall Field.

OPPOSITE TOP The Painted Room, Mr. and Mrs. John Magee residence (Pebble Beach, California), 1930, with boiserie in salmon, gray, cream and beige reinstalled from a French château. *Town & Country* wrote in October 1932 that "the impression given is that you are standing within a huge iridescent soap bubble."

OPPOSITE BOTTOM Living room, Hillyer Brown residence (Hillsborough, California), 1937. Frances' simple decor included sofas covered in cotton chintz and an antique French chaise longue covered in a quilted modern fabric.

ABOVE Boudoir, John Chapman residence (Pebble Beach, California), 1938. The walls are in a green-and-white Swedish linen. The curtains are neatly encased in pockets under the wall covering. Other details include a brush-fringed chaise longue, a modern revolving bookstand with a Chinese fretwork detail, and an off-white shag carpet.

OPPOSITE Penthouse library, Joseph Ryerson residence (Chicago, Illinois), 1930. The first known instance of Frances incorporating the style of Jean-Michel Frank, the handsomely modern 24-by-40-foot library was fitted out by David Adler. Frances is believed to have designed the seating based on Frank forms. A long, cushioned sofa with rounded arms—so big it had to be made in the room—matching lounge chairs, a U-shaped Frank parchment side table, his Waterfall low table and Ball table lamps were some of the furnishings. Striped upholstery was closely related to the enormous zebra skins laid over the parquet floor. Adler also designed the frames of white wood with inner borders of mirrored glass.

and interior designer Jean-Michel Frank (1895–1941) was a major influence on Frances's style. Frank's elegantly spare furniture, comprised of exotic and unusual materials, as well as his ethic of sober refinement and a serene absence of clutter were important elements in many of Frances's rooms starting in the 1930s.

Frank took under his wing a stable of stellar talents, including the sculptor Alberto Giacometti and his brother Diego Giacometti, and the furniture designers Emilio Terry and Paul Rodocanachi, all of whose designs Frances would regularly use.

Along with Frank's own designs, Alberto Giacometti's beautifully sculpted white plaster lamps, wall lights, vases, and mirror frames frequently found a place in Frances's interiors. While heavily patronizing Frank's studio, Frances also bought extravagant beds, tables and plaster palm-tree torchieres designed by the French designer and artist Serge Roche, and ultra-refined custom furniture from the Paris workrooms of Maison Jansen.

During this time, Frances began to decorate homes designed by two California architects of the emerging "Second Bay Tradition" style, Gardner Dailey and William Wurster, allowing her to work in modernist California homes for the first time. She first collaborated with the California-born Wurster (1895–1973) in the early 1930s, furnishing his simple board-and-batten weekend ranch houses in the golf community of Pasatiempo, and more substantial homes for the elite on the San Francisco Peninsula. Before he embraced modernism in his designs starting in 1936, Dailey (1895–1967) was known as a master at creating period-style homes in the English, Spanish, French or early American manner. Like Adler, Dailey had a highly tuned sense of proportion.

Frances decorated as many as forty homes, hotels and clubs built by Dailey, and he was ultimately her most frequent architect collaborator. In contrast to the more rustic vernacular style of Wurster, "The houses of Gardner Dailey are contemporary in feeling but marked by an elegance and an infinite attention to detail which set them apart from the run-of-the-mill modern."[5]

One of Frances's 1936 projects was decorating Dailey's own home. Columnist Herb Caen of the *San Francisco Chronicle* reported that "One of the most notable apartments on Telegraph Hill is that designed and occupied by Gardner A. Dailey, the top-flight architect; for sheer luxury, exquisite taste and majesty of view, this dream house on Telegraph Hill boulevard can't be touched."

Frances began her association with California weaver Dorothy Liebes (1897–1972) in about 1936. Frances was ahead of the curve in realizing that Liebes's brightly colored hand-woven fabrics with their unusual blends of yarns, metallic threads, reeds and other materials represented a whole new frontier of textile design.

During this time, Frances also began to purchase furniture and fabrics designed by the English decorator Syrie Maugham (1879–1955), as well as antiques selected from Syrie's English and American shops. The women are

ABOVE LEFT Study, Jean-Michel Frank apartment, rue de Verneuil (Paris, France), circa 1931, in a photo owned by Frances Elkins.

ABOVE, RIGHT TOP TO BOTTOM Jean-Michel Frank, portrait by Man Ray, 1927. Chinese Pillow lamp on a mica coffee table, both designed by Frank, in a photo from Chanaux & Co. owned by Frances.

OPPOSITE, CLOCKWISE FROM TOP LEFT Dolphin table designed by Syrie Maugham, photographed at the Robert Louis Stevenson House. Antique wing chair Frances acquired from Syrie Maugham. A drawing of Syrie Maugham, artist unknown, from *The Bystander*, January 15, 1935. Samples of Syrie Maugham fabrics from the Frances Elkins archives.

believed to have collaborated or worked simultaneously on a few 1930s projects, most notably the home of Celia Tobin Clark. Frances appreciated the sense of romantic exuberance and plush feminine glamour in Syrie's interiors, as well as her ability to express the modernist mood.

Despite the onset of the Great Depression, Frances had her hands full with more than commissions as the 1930s began, including country houses, apartments, hotels, and private clubs. Her accomplishments in 1930 alone were extraordinary.[6]

Frances's reputation had spread to the East Coast by the 1930s, and her New York clients included the Barbizon-Plaza Hotel and Evelyn Marshall Field, who had Frances and Adler design her River House apartment

just as work was being completed on Mrs. Field's Long Island residence.

In 1938, Frances hired the British-born LeGrande "Lee" Dix as her Man Friday. Dix remained with Elkins for the remainder of her career, supervising her installations, building furniture, doing upholstery and creating accessories. Dix would make decorative giltwood or ebonized boxes inspired by boxes designed by Alberto Giacometti for Jean-Michel Frank.

During her summer sojourns to a rented Venetian palazzo with its stunning view of the Grand Canal, Frances entertained friends such as Coco Chanel, Salvador Dali, Charles de Beistegui, Elsa Schiaparelli, and Jose and Misia Sert. Chanel would visit Frances in Monterey in 1931.

At the end of the decade, Frances's reputation as a leading American designer was solidly established, as noted in an editorial in the *Monterey Peninsula Herald*. "There are two or three names that are mentioned in the United States as the leading personages in the field of interior decoration. Mrs. Elkins' is one of those names. It is a name also among the decorators in France, who fashion any number of things in her order, that may be seen in California, in New York, in Florida, and in homes elsewhere. And in Monterey, it is a name among craftsmen who create to her exacting specifications furniture that is destined for homes far distant from California, among craftswomen who carry out her design of draperies."[7] •

OPPOSITE TOP Main lounge, San Francisco Building, Golden Gate International Exposition, 1939. Clarence Tantau was the architect. Dorothy Liebes designed the banded yellow-string draperies. The main lounge featured natural-colored wood-veneer walls and mammoth seven-foot-tall palm-form gilded aluminum chandeliers with matching wall lights.

OPPOSITE BOTTOM Dining room, William Paley townhouse, New York City, decorated circa 1935. A fireplace with bolection molding, silvered wall panels, a Serge Roche mirrored console, and an oval cut-pile rug likely designed by Marion Dorn are on display. The dining chairs may have been designed by Frances.

RIGHT TOP Terrace, Joseph Cudahy residence, Lake Forest, Illinois (1930). This colorized postcard shows the outdoor furniture, planters, and awnings against the French Norman–style house of square-cut Lannon stone.

RIGHT BOTTOM Lounge, Coral Casino aka Biltmore Beach Club (Montecito, California), 1937. Gardner Dailey designed the Coral Casino, a private membership beach. The aquatic mural was possibly painted by Jane Berlandina (the casino has no record of the artist). The mural was covered over and forgotten for several decades until it was discovered and restored during a recent renovation.

Del Monte Lodge

PEBBLE BEACH, CALIFORNIA · 1930–1935

IN 1930, FRANCES WAS hired to redecorate the Del Monte Lodge, rebuilt in 1919 after a fire destroyed the original log cabin–style structure. It was natural that Samuel F.B. Morse's Del Monte Properties Company, which had hired Frances to decorate the Hotel Del Monte starting in 1926, would turn to her to renovate its smaller inn a few years later. Morse, a friend and client, would write in his unpublished memoirs that when it came to decorating, "[I]t is my humble opinion that there is nobody in her class in that field."

A 1919 brochure noted that the "bijou hotel . . . presents a place of complete comfort and luxury for . . . guests, and also serves as a clubhouse and social rendezvous for those whose homes are adjacent." Two stories tall, in a style that might be called Palladian Mediterranean, the lodge had expansive public rooms including lounges, a dining room, tearoom (later a card room), grill, and 55 guest rooms.

French provincial antiques, scenic wallpaper, and chandeliers were some of the Gallic components of Frances's 1930 schemes, which also featured English, American, Asian and Polynesian influences. Frances realized that French-country furnishings, when compared with the more formal French court-type furniture, imparted a sense of rusticity and pared-down simplicity that made the interiors seem more comfortable and hospitable.

A 1930 advertisement for Daggett & Ramsell's Perfect Cold Cream—"provided in the dressing rooms of the exclusive Lodge"—described life there "as vivid and varied as a story book." The ad also touted that the lodge hosted "distinguished guests from all over the world—titled Europeans, American industrial and social leaders, authors, and artists and actors."

The treatment Frances gave the lodge reflected her mastery of what writer Dupuy Warrick Reed in his 1984 *Connoisseur* profile of Elkins called the "sophisticated country" style, mixing a down-home American informality with European chic. •

ABOVE Gene McComas's *Polynesian Trilogy* murals, which were set into panels in the dining room. Expatriate writer and native Californian Gertrude Stein commented on a visit to the lodge: "This is the finest art I have seen since coming to America."

OPPOSITE FROM TOP The main dining room was marked by the brightly colored murals, orange walls, and massive palm-form chandeliers, mixed with pale-green dining chairs. A 1939 Lodge brochure succinctly noted that "[t]he dining room. . . is especially beautiful." Mrs. Samuel F. B. Morse in 1935 sitting between investment banker Henry D. Phelps (at left) and Edward S. Hillman Jr., heir to a Chicago department store fortune.

LEFT Four color Curt Teich postcards believed to accurately depict Frances's decor. From top: The dining room. The Monkeyshines Room, also known as the Monkey Room, was a cocktail lounge Frances designed after the end of Prohibition in 1933. The murals, created by Phil Nesbitt, a former Disney Studios cartoonist, depicted inebriated monkeys engaging in "monkeyshines." According to Anne Germain's nostalgic 1975 *Pebble Beach: The Way It Was*: "Great fun was had in the Monkey Room, sometimes followed by or preceded by dinner in the Main Zoo, as the dining room was called," "Salvador Dali was once observed munching a daisy in the Monkey Room." Frances configured the Terrace Lounge as a comfortable living room, with multiple seating areas and game tables, and a pleasing combination of furniture—curved and square seating, bulky with the delicate. The room was anchored at one end by a capacious French provincial armoire. Its color scheme was keyed to Pueblos, two canvases of New Mexico cliff dwellers by local artist Francis McComas. One can be seen over the fireplace. The Indian Room took its name from the room's French scenic wallpaper, Hindustan, by Jean Zuber. The painted mantel, wainscoting, and door echo the blues in the panoramic paper. Comfortable upholstered sofas in red, English Regency-style chairs in rose used at French provincial card tables, and countrified Pembroke tables create an atmosphere of relaxation amid refinement.

OPPOSITE TOP The Terrace Lounge with its original furnishings appeared in the 1956 thriller *Julie*. Actress Doris Day can be seen running through the lounge in one early scene.

OPPOSITE BOTTOM Two guests in golfing attire chatting in the Terrace Lounge, circa 1935. Elizabeth and George Coleman Jr. of Oklahoma at a game table in the Terrace Lounge, in 1936, on their first visit to the Monterey Peninsula. They would hire Frances to decorate their Oklahoma residence and, ten years later, their new home in Pebble Beach.

Mr. & Mrs. Wolcott Blair

CHICAGO, ILLINOIS · 1931

LIKE MANY FRANCES ELKINS designs, Wolcott and Ellen Blair's Chicago residence was praised at the time for its skillful blending of the traditional and the modern. The 1931 decor is significant not only by itself, but for how Frances's schemes for the Blair townhouse would figure into a much more famous address of the couple: Villa Blair in Palm Beach, decorated by Ruby Ross Wood in 1936, which is considered a landmark of 20th-century interior design.

Between 1915 and 1917, David Adler and his partner, Henry Corwith Dangler, designed four handsome Georgian-style rowhouses on Lakeview Avenue in Chicago. These units were first occupied by socially prominent friends of the architects, including artist Abram Poole, architect Ambrose Cramer (Dangler's cousin), and widowed *Titanic* survivor Mrs. Joseph Ryerson. Dangler would also own one of the homes.

The Wolcott Blairs bought the three-story Ryerson unit in 1930. They hired Adler to renovate the townhouse. Frances would handle the decoration. The interiors would soon be featured in several pages in *Arts & Decoration* magazine, and the dining room would be profiled over two pages in *Town & Country*.

"The decoration is restrained throughout," noted *Arts & Decoration* in December 1933. "In these rooms, the present-day spirit plays with the best of the other periods." A&D also remarked how Elkins was able to achieve "... the contemporary feeling for simplicity, for fitting the furnishings into the whole design." •

ABOVE AND OPPOSITE The dining room's theme was predominantly English, with modern touches, as shown in these two 1932 images. Delicately paneled white-plaster walls were the envelope for this striking room. Queen Anne chairs slipcovered in a silvery-white satin with thin black zigzags were set around an English pedestal table. Syrie Maugham supplied the modern Marion Dorn rug, its cut pile and chenille pattern echoing a Greek key design. The carpet was described as "undyed, natural black sheeps' [sic] wool" by August Owen Patterson in a 1932 *Town & Country*. She remarked how the rug was "advantageously used on the dark polished wood floor." A pair of ebony mirrored screens designed by Maugham were placed on either side of the Adam fireplace. The dining room was exactly re-created in Palm Beach—the architecture, light fixtures, fireplace, floor, furnishings, rugs, and all decorations. The Blairs sold their Chicago home one year after finishing Villa Blair.

OPPOSITE A 1932 view of the drawing room, which, according to *Arts & Decoration*, "purposefully draws a more luxurious note," noting that Frances did not overextend the "Chinese feeling" represented in the room's artwork, jade, and cloisonné. A "less thoughtful decorator," they wrote, would have used Chinese Chippendale furniture. The slipcovered chairs, burl wood chests, and other pieces would be reused by Ruby Ross Wood in the library at Villa Blair.

ABOVE Mrs. Blair's Palm Beach bedroom decorated by Ruby Ross Wood. Several components had been transported from two Chicago rooms Frances decorated, mostly with the same textiles, including the two Syrie Maugham tufted loveseats in beige velvet at the foot of the bed and the Aubusson rug.

LEFT Designer Mark Hampton's 1993 painting of the beige-and-white Villa Blair drawing room decorated by Ruby Ross Wood.

Mr. & Mrs. Lester Armour

LAKE BLUFF, ILLINOIS · 1931–1936

MEAT-PACKING HEIR Lester Armour and his wife, Leola (née Stanton), gave their David Adler–designed house the name "Chateau d'Aigle" (House of the Eagle). Fittingly, the house had eagle designs in several rooms. Though rooted in formal English and eastern American traditions, the forty-six-room mansion had an easygoing 20th-century air. Chateau d'Aigle was a user-friendly family home and was as accommodating for the children as for their parents (and the family dogs). "It's pure, unostentatious splendor," wrote Paul Galloway in a 1987 *Chicago Tribune* feature on the house.

The Georgian-style mansion was built of a whitewashed yellow brick and situated at the end of a long allée with a monumental canopy of tall elm trees. Hammond-Harwood House in Maryland was Adler's primary inspiration for the center block of the house. Two-story wings on either side contained guest rooms and staff quarters.

Frances was able to compose suitably impressive rooms that were simultaneously gracious and uncomplicated. For the majestic gallery that set the tone for the house, Frances added three graceful hanging lanterns in a bell jar shape embellished by crystal (or possibly cut-glass) drops supplied by the firm of Edward F. Caldwell. The elliptical gallery with a black-and-white marble floor led to the main staircase and the dining room at its opposite end. One of a pair of custom commodes was surmounted by a large urn. Figurative statuary is set in twin niches above a pair of white leather neoclassical benches, near a settee in the same style. Writing about the gallery in his 1970 book *David Adler: The Architect and His Work,* Richard Pratt effused that "[t]he ceiling, fourteen feet high, together with the white walls and woodwork, gives a marvelously free and airy feeling."

Among her many influences, Frances was not afraid to absorb current trends in art and design as evidenced by Mrs. Armour's stunning Art Deco bathroom/dressing room. The bath was fitted out with mirrored panels framed with molded bands of mirror, a white marble tub, and a mirrored dressing table inset under a window. The sleek black marble floor was patterned with a finely scaled metal inlay of stripes with a trellis and leaf motif. The beaded ceiling light was from Maison Baguès. Then a *House & Garden* editor, New York architect James Shearron attempted, to no avail, to interest the Art Institute of Chicago in rescuing the dressing room when it was going to be removed from the house by a subsequent owner. Decorator Miles Redd eventually acquired the room through a salvage company and reinstalled it in his own New York home. The room has also been memorialized in *A Wedding,* a 1978 film by Robert Altman.

In 1941, *Chicago Daily Tribune* columnist Cousin Eve declared the house a "Georgian gem overlooking the lake with a charming interior." •

OPPOSITE One end of the long gallery across the center of the house in a rare colorized stereo card from the 1930s. Pale celadon walls were decorated with friezes of repeating images, originally taken from an old Federal pattern. Vertical bands of palm fronds were hand-painted onto the design.

ABOVE The exterior of the Armour house.

LEFT The dining room's leather-covered Hepplewhite–style armchairs were from Frank Partridge & Sons. A twelve-panel Coromandel screen was divided and placed on either side of a mahogany sideboard. The tall crystal chandelier was said to be from a Hapsburg palace in Austria.

LEFT BELOW The bright morning room, or breakfast room. Panels of a rare scenic wallpaper were purchased in Europe and augmented by painted panels. An Aubusson-style rug complemented the wallpaper.

OPPOSITE TOP The ultraglamorous Art Deco dressing room.

OPPOSITE BOTTOM LEFT Richer, deeper tones in the library gave it a warm ambience. The English pine paneling came from a library in Europe. Several of the tables were purposely mismatched to make the room seem less stuffy, as if the furniture were put together by the owners at random.

OPPOSITE BOTTOM RIGHT The cheerful living porch with garden was decorated in blue and white, Frances's favorite color combination.

Mr. & Mrs. Edison Dick

LAKE FOREST, ILLINOIS · 1932–1935

IN 1932, THE YOUNG Edison and Jane (née Warner) Dick had David Adler design their relatively modest home facing a ravine in Lake Forest, Illinois. Adler would later add a guest wing in 1935. Edison Dick was an executive of the A.B. Dick Company, which was founded by his father. The company, still in existence, was responsible for inventing the mimeograph machine.

Architecturally, the Dick residence has been described variously as pure colonial revival or in the style of the Greek Revival and is said to be inspired by the Baldwin-Buss House in Hudson, Ohio. The facade was painted a bright white, with contrast afforded by dark-green shutters. The exterior and the interior both had classical Greek detailing, including window frames and grilles in Greek fretwork patterns, a pale-toned powder room with gold Greek frets on the doors, and a corresponding fret motif bordering a circular rug.

The easygoing traditional interiors Frances created for the Edison Dicks demonstrated her ability to work on a more intimate scale. In keeping with her usual themes of comfort and simplicity, Frances outfitted the rooms in the house using mostly English antiques, many of which were purchased overseas by the couple themselves, mixed with new furniture of her own design and some French influences. •

ABOVE FROM TOP One of the Chinese Chippendale mural designs for the primary bathroom. A sample of the red toile de Jouy pattern used in the guest bedroom.

OPPOSITE TOP In the modest-size living room, custom spruce-paneled walls impart an up-to-the-minute spareness. The mantel was designed by Robert Adam. Adler's design of Gothic Revival bookcases was another nod to English architecture.

OPPOSITE BOTTOM, FROM LEFT The simplicity of the dining room's decor and architecture is readily apparent. There was no chandelier as the Dicks preferred to dine by candlelight. In the primary bedroom, a blue and off-white glazed cotton fabric of flowers, branch forms, birds, and butterflies covered the lushly fringed canopy bed, curtains, and walls. In the guest bedroom, Frances covered twin beds in a red-and-ecru cotton toile de Jouy that she had hand-quilted in her workshops. The beds were trimmed with ball fringe (including three rows of the fringe on the skirting). Frances designed the cushioned club chair in the corner.

Cypress Point Clubhouse

PEBBLE BEACH, CALIFORNIA · 1930

FOR THE HANDSOME CLUBHOUSE of the exclusive Cypress Point Club, Frances created quietly welcoming environments through a conscientious use of color and designed for a balance of friendly commonality and reserve. Completed in 1930, the clubhouse was the final project for Santa Barbara architect George Washington Smith. In 1931 *California Arts & Architecture* described the structure as a "simple and charming adaptation of the old Monterey dwelling," recognizing its roots in the Monterey colonial style known for a second-floor balcony and hip roof. Smith, like David Adler, had a remarkable sense of scale, which lent Frances a perfect background for her own compositions. The clubhouse interiors were timeless.

The brilliance of Frances's furniture plan for the club room included an enormous French provincial map table at center with seating groups around fireplaces at either end. A third seating area was created by a sofa placed along the wall opposite the French doors. The room was spacious enough to allow a sense of separation for small parties wanting privacy, yet the furniture arrangement facilitated a smooth flow when used for large gatherings.

The amply cushioned armchairs were covered in a brown tweed fabric, while Port Arlington sofas and large provincial bergères were upholstered in orange velvet, an example of Frances's ability to mix contrasting textures harmoniously. The yellow linen curtains were trimmed with brown-and-cream fringe and tassels. Myron Oliver, Frances's cabinetmaker, copied Directoire furniture from a French château to make the bridge chairs and tables. Oliver also made the French provincial–style coffee tables with black-marble tops. Brass chandeliers were hung near each of the fireplaces, while white craquelure Chinese vases were fashioned into table lamps. The tall French provincial secretary echoes the door heights.

"The effect is that of a discriminating private residence, rather than the usual 'clubhouse' or hotel atmosphere," *Game & Gossip* reported in 1931. They also praised the decor's "good taste and refinement." •

OPPOSITE TOP A circa 1949 photo.

OPPOSITE BOTTOM The black-and-white image shows how Frances decorated the room in the early 1930s.

ABOVE FROM TOP Framed by windswept Monterey cypresses, the rear of the white-painted clubhouse with its green shutters is shown in a 1930s postcard. This hallway highlights Frances's penchant for imported wallpapers, here The Fables of La Fontaine by Dufour. The chair and the star-form colonial-style chandelier are original to the decor.

ABOVE The grand simplicity of the club room was balanced by a brighter color palette of green and white in the dining room, shown in a 1950s view.

RIGHT Paul Winslow and Frances Elkins on the Cypress Point golf course in 1932. She was then one of the few single women club members. Frances wore couture Chanel golfing costumes with blouse cuffs she could button onto her coats or sweaters.

OPPOSITE TOP A 1930s image of the ladies dressing room, which *Arts & Architecture* pronounced "dainty rather than elaborate. Excellent taste was shown in the furnishing." The wallpaper in a small-scale print was white and gold. Orange moiré covered the sofa and three stools.

OPPOSITE BOTTOM The four upstairs bedrooms were named after women club members. Each suite had a distinct color motif—yellow and green; blue; plum; and, red and ecru.

Mrs. Celia Tobin Clark

HILLSBOROUGH, CALIFORNIA · 1929–1936

(WITH SYRIE MAUGHAM)

HOUSE ON HILL, THE RAMBLING San Francisco Peninsula country home of banking heiress Celia Tobin Clark, was one of David Adler's most celebrated achievements and certainly his largest and most important job in the West. Adler designed the house in a hybrid of English styles: the one-and-a-half-story entrance elevation in a more Georgian character and the more widely photographed three-story rear Tudor facade. His concept for the home was inspired by the English country houses of Sir Edwin L. Lutyens.

Mrs. Clark was the daughter of Richard Tobin, one of the founders of the Hibernia Bank of San Francisco. From 1904 to 1925, she was married to Charles W. Clark, whose father, Senator William Clark of Montana, was a copper magnate and at one time the second wealthiest man in the U.S. Charles Clark and Felton Elkins played polo together, and Frances knew Mrs. Clark as early as 1918.

The extent of Frances's involvement in the Clark house has been somewhat of a mystery, but new clues have emerged to clarify Frances's substantial role in the decor. While Frances's project files for the Clark house are lost, what has been found recently in her archives are congenial 1936 letters between Celia and Frances (they were on a first-name basis) that documented the ongoing decor as well as Casa Blanca bank deposit records and ledger book entries for Mrs. Clark from 1929 through 1931. Also, Frances had pasted the illustrated pages from *Town & Country*'s February 1953 house feature into her scrapbook, "Houses of David Adler and Frances Elkins."

Some rooms in particular bear Frances's unmistakable style. While the decor for Mrs. Clark's bedroom, for example, has been attributed to Syrie Maugham alone, there are hints that it was quite possibly a collaboration with Frances. Overall, the composition is more strictly tailored and symmetrical than any other room Syrie had designed; such crispness was very much Frances's signature. Conceivably, Syrie supplied the concept, and some of the furniture, perhaps, and Frances helped her finesse

it. There was a commonality of taste between the two women: Frances often relied upon Syrie to supply fabrics, furniture, and lamps for her various jobs. It seems plausible that Frances assisted Syrie, in faraway London, in executing her vision for Mrs. Clark's bedroom.

And a 1936 handwritten letter from Mrs. Clark to Frances about a pair of gold-painted plaster Jean-Michel Frank table lamps in the Music Room raved: "I want you to see the Frank lamps which couldn't possibly be more successful."

It was known that Adler accompanied Mrs. Clark to England to shop for antiques for the home in summer 1929 and that he introduced Mrs. Clark to Syrie Maugham. And newspaper accounts have established that Frances was in Europe from spring to winter 1929, making it likely she joined the shopping expeditions. •

ABOVE The three-story rear elevation. In his 1970 monograph on Adler, Richard Pratt wrote that "[t]his façade may easily be one of Adler's greatest."

OPPOSITE A never-published 1950 photo of the long reception gallery on the entrance level, which established the predominantly English temperament of the interiors.

ABOVE The 55-foot-long music room was lined with locally carved panels of Engelmann spruce. The patterned plaster ceiling featured garlands, rosettes, and musical instruments. Frances, in her presumed role as lead decorator, integrated English and French antiques with the Chinese. She added some French modernist touches a few years later. The appealing mix of fine furniture of various heights was arranged to create a feeling of intimacy while honoring the majesty of the room. A noted music and arts patron, Mrs. Clark was also an amateur musician.

ABOVE, FROM TOP Tony Duquette's circa-1950 color slides provide more visual information and show the layering of detailing throughout. In the center image, Frances's close friend Mrs. Edmunds Lyman perches on a fringed lavender wing chair near a Giacometti gilded floor lamp and a Jean-Michel Frank Croisillon table lamp. The slides also reveal the textile colors: the tawny fabric on the Queen Anne shepherd's-crook armchairs; the reds, burgundies, blues, and oranges used in the upholstery, rugs, and curtains; and the blue accents of the Chinese porcelain.

RIGHT The exquisite dining room was perfectly furnished to set off the grandeur of the architecture. The circa-1760 Chinese wallpaper, possibly called Flowers, Birds, and Insects, was purchased by David Adler in Venice.

FOLLOWING Views of Mrs. Clark's famous bedroom, including two color images by Tony Duquette, circa 1950. Mark Hampton called the bedroom "a high point in the design of the thirties"; it still has a wide following among design aficionados. The wallcovering was a white linen with a stenciled scroll pattern believed to be based on an 18th-century Swedish design. Frances's records only identify it as a "Swedish linen."

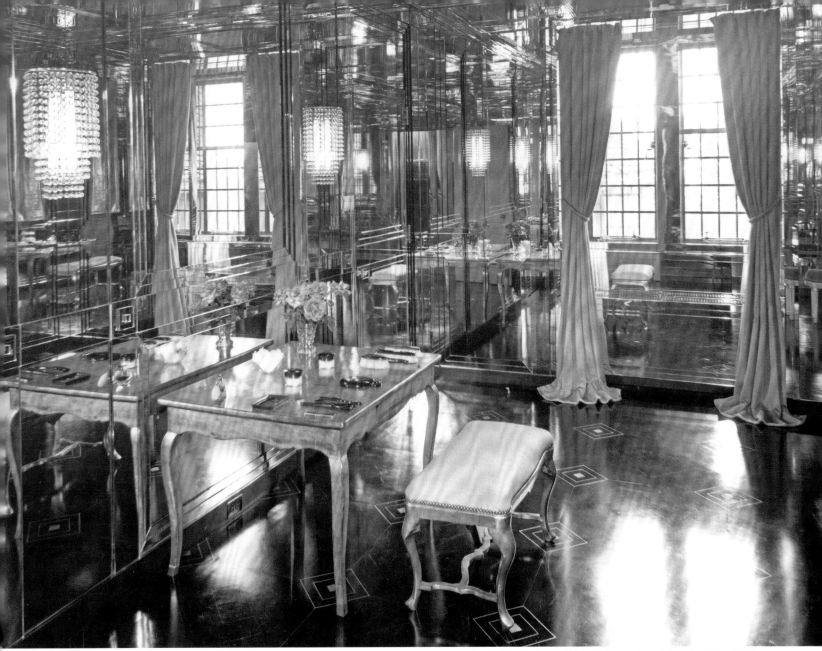

OPPOSITE TOP *Connoisseur* featured the library in its 1958 book *100 Most Beautiful Rooms in America*, lauding its "pleasant atmosphere of restfulness," owing to the absence of patterned fabrics, rugs, and curtains. The valances are of a recognizable Syrie Maugham design, and it is believed that Frances and Syrie collaborated on the design of this room.

OPPOSITE BOTTOM Left, A late-1940s Jerome Zerbe photo of Mrs. Clark entertaining guests in the library, which had fifteen-foot ceilings. Right, old pine paneling, fine antiques, and an inviting color scheme of greens and beiges gave the library its warm ambience.

ABOVE This simple women's dressing room is classic Frances Elkins. She used identical beaded Baguès wall sconces in several other projects, and the silvered dressing table bench is similar to other Elkins designs. The curtains puddle on the floor, a look Frances strongly preferred in homes she decorated in the 1930s.

RIGHT The Chinese wallpaper from the guest bedroom, whose walls were painted a light aqua blue; a slightly deeper blue was used on doors and trim, repeating colors found in the wallpaper.

Mrs. Carolyn Morse Ely

CHICAGO, ILLINOIS · 1930–1934

THE MAGNIFICENT APARTMENT that Frances created for Mrs. Carolyn Morse Ely was one of Frances's masterpieces. The glory of the design, with interior architecture by David Adler, is how Frances juxtaposed antique elements into interiors that were concisely contemporary.

After selling her Lake Bluff country house in 1928, Mrs. Ely was one of the buyers in a new sixteen-story Art Deco limestone cooperative apartment building designed by architect Philip Maher and completed in 1929. For the two-level Chicago apartment, Frances would repurpose several pieces of furniture from Lake Bluff—for example, the dining table and Louis XV–style chairs—working them into rooms with a more effusive modern style.

One of Frances's boldest early projects, the Ely apartment was a cosmopolitan vision of urbanity and glamour that could only have been put together by someone with broad global experience. A well-traveled and extremely sophisticated American, Frances as a decorator had a vast range of resources that made her unique for her time.

For example, in Paris Frances had recently been exposed to the work of Jean-Michel Frank. His restrained aesthetic likely inspired her to design an envelope of the plainest wood for Mrs. Ely's living room. Seamless natural-toned wood paneling on the walls and a tented ceiling created a sense of tranquility and calm in the room.

And the mixing of Chinese furniture and bibelots with French, English, and modern furnishings reflects both women's interest in Asian antiques. Mrs. Ely was one of the first directors of The Oriental, a society for people interested in Asian art formed at the Art Institute in 1925.

In a 1930 letter, Mrs. Potter Palmer, Mrs. Ely's upstairs neighbor and a client of Frances's, wrote: "Carrie Ely's flat is the most brilliant—quite modern backgrounds with old furniture."

Frances was evidently proud of her work on the Ely apartment, as she framed eight photos of the interiors to hang in her office. (The images here were scanned from those photos.) •

ABOVE Frances used reflective materials in the dining room to create a big-city atmosphere. Exotic palm wallpaper painted beige and silver and underpinned with an etched mirror dado in strips of gold, silver, and black glass was countered with the cool sobriety of embossed metal double doors. Mrs. Palmer wrote that the room was "entirely modern, in brown and silver, and quite exciting and entirely indescribable!"

OPPOSITE The quiet austerity of a downstairs corridor is juxtaposed with the sense of fantasy in the dining room, seen through the doorway. Elongated ultramodern steel-and-glass sconces from E.F. Caldwell light the passageway.

OPPOSITE Frances used furniture in varying heights in the living room to achieve her trademark symmetry. Neutral-shaded wood provided a sense of spaciousness. The modern sofa in brown with gold highlights, recycled from Lake Bluff, faces a fringed English wing chair and a Louis XVI-style chair in dark wood. Rectilinear lines are balanced with curvilinear forms. The white Jean-Michel Frank table lamp adds a modernist note. The crystal wall lights are by Maison Baguès.

RIGHT TOP Imposing carved pelmets raise the eye toward the ceiling, while black marble baseboards set off the grain of the floor. A settee covered in a tan-and-silver silk fabric with a raised zigzag pattern commands the window seating area.

RIGHT BOTTOM A circa 18th-century Chinese framed mural hangs over a country table covered with decorative Chinese ceramics and pottery.

FOLLOWING Mrs. Ely's bedroom, with its tall ceilings, had a similar sense of drama as the living room. The walls were covered in silver paper. The furnishings were also silvered, including the silver-gray curtains.

Mrs. Kersey Coates Reed

LAKE FOREST, ILLINOIS · 1929–1932

THE MRS. KERSEY COATES REED house represents Elkins at her apogee. The commission is considered the pinnacle of the country-house collaborations with her brother, David Adler. The much-celebrated 32,000-square-foot Georgian Revival home was decorated in an innovative fusion of traditional and Art Deco. A setting for many fine English and French antiques, the residence also featured at least five rooms in the luxuriously spare Jean-Michel Frank style. The tennis house was in itself a masterpiece of understated elegance. Adler's disciplined and stately interior and exterior architecture has also been highly praised for the Palladian layout of the main house and two adjoining wings.

"The chicest house in America" is how New York architect James Shearron described the residence. Shearron, of the 2022 AD 100 firm Bories & Shearron, goes on: "It's the combination of juxtapositions that makes it shocking and dramatic. A Pennsylvania stone country house, meant to be humble, but laid out like a Palladian house. Then you step inside—it's *glamorous*. . . . It takes a dip into the 'wow factor' in many rooms. But enough of them added together, and then the *depth* of them all. Plus the *tennis house*—there's

more!" Shearron was raised in Lake Forest and had visited the Reed house when it had its original decor.

Helen Shedd Reed was the daughter of John Shedd, president of Marshall Field & Company, then the most prestigious Chicago department store. Mrs. Reed was widowed when her husband, attorney Kersey Coates Reed, died suddenly in 1929. But she proceeded with their plans to build the summer house, which she would occupy with her children, John and Mary. •

OPPOSITE The elegantly sinuous stairway, sparkling with light, as seen from the gallery. The treads and handrails are ebony. Innovatively, Frances used modern industrial glass for the spindles. Based on family lore and its use elsewhere in the house, the spindles are believed to be Steuben.

ABOVE Left, an exterior view. In 1941, the *Chicago Daily Tribune* reported that "the residence presents an almost austere effect, but once within, formality mellows into a feeling of gracious hospitality." Right, the capacious 16-by-40-foot gallery was an arresting study in high contrast, with off-white walls and a black-and-white marble floor with furnishings in the same key.

OPPOSITE The ladies' powder room mixed Art Deco with paneling and furnishings based on historical English precedents. Sheets of heavy Steuben were set in paneled walls of lacquered yellow edged with silver leaf. The black-and-gold dressing table is a Queen Anne model Frances used in numerous projects. Frances bought the yellow Bessarabian rug in London.

ABOVE For the men's dressing room, Frances asked Jean-Michel Frank to help carry out her vision for a whitewashed room. All the furnishings were designed by Frank and his associates, the Giacometti brothers and Paul Rodocanachi. A bas-relief by Alberto Giacometti hangs above a simple Frank fireplace of white plaster bordered by small blocks of gypsum that give the effect of rock crystal.

ABOVE AND OPPOSITE Decorated in shades of brown with green accents, the handsome living room was filled with high-quality English furnishings and Asian accessories. Frances bought the glazed chintz in London to cover the overstuffed sofas and armchairs. The original fabric (opposite, top) was a white floral pattern with green leaves on a brown background. The tasseled and fringed curtains were brown serge. A rich green leather was applied to the Queen Anne armchairs. Wing chairs placed in two corners were upholstered in a pale green with brown fringe. A pair of Han dynasty pottery

jars in a dark brownish-green glaze were made into the lamps by the fireside, with cream-glazed Tang period vases used for the lamps by the windows. Benches in a vivid green were positioned by the hearth. Chinese fluorite objects in jade green ornament the mantel. Karabagh tapestry panels covered the French parquet floors. August Owen Patterson explained that Frances "[b]leached the bright colors out of old rugs so they would have quiet wood tones." A mahogany breakfront bookcase lined the wall. A splendid cut-glass chandelier cast indirect lighting from inside, with the cups holding real candles.

ABOVE The white-painted north and south halls each contained seating areas. The sofas and chairs in a green-and-white glazed chintz were trimmed in ruffled skirts (a "flounce"), a style Frances would often use. The fabric detail (at right) is from a book documenting the home's textiles given to Mrs. Reed by Frances after the house was completed. The ebonized-oak floor has Monel Metal inserts to form a geometric pattern. The low table with eggshell-and-lacquer finish was created by the Swiss artist and sculptor Jean Dunand.

OPPOSITE The dining room was an homage to the Chinese Chippendale style. The hand-painted wallpaper was antique. The pattern on the wool rugs by Marion Dorn suggests Chinese fretwork. The curtains were a tawny gold silk; a wing chair in the breakfast bay was similarly covered. Waterford sconces provided the electric lighting.

ABOVE AND OPPOSITE What Mark Hampton called "the most boldly stylish room" in America, the Reed library has also been called Frances's most remarkable design. Frances brought together the talents of her brother, as well as Jean-Michel Frank and Adolph Chanaux, to realize a stunning statement of understated modernism. Augusta Owen Patterson wrote: "One of the quietest rooms in the house is the most radical in its departure from custom."

Frances covered walls and cornices with parchment-colored Hermès goatskin, hand-sewn in Paris, with welted seams to suggest paneling. Segments of stripped ornate pine woodwork from Grove House in Surrey were used for the mantel, doors, and door surrounds on the fireplace wall. The recessed bookshelves were filled with books in complementary brown leather and off-white bindings. Frances had whole shelves of books covered in parchment, with only their titles visible. Between the bookcases are a Frank-designed leather Comfortable sofa and a low mica coffee table with a tortoiseshell finish. The light-colored curtains were of a heavy wool weave supplied by Chanaux and matched the wing chairs. They puddled on the floor at the tall French doors, accentuating the room's height.

Three Karabagh tapestry panels were laid over the antique French parquetry floor. Frances had the rugs bleached to harmonize with the leather walls and the room's buff and brown tones. Asian art pieces were employed as decor, including a Qing dynasty ancestor portrait.

OPPOSITE Mrs. Reed's bedroom was elegantly restrained in basically a two-color scheme of cream and green. The simple glaze-painted paneled walls were cream colored, with gold detailing. A large cream-colored rug covered the parquet floors. The heavily fringed chaise longue and bed were covered in a glazed and quilted lily-of-the-valley fabric (seen above) with a cream background and white flowers edged in brown with leaves in deep green and light blue.

RIGHT The bedroom walls of Mrs. Reed's daughter, Mary, were covered in a hand-painted Chinese wallpaper in ivory and blue, supplying the room's color scheme. The room's centerpiece was the Regency-style tester bed by Syrie Maugham. The bedposts were carved faux bamboo tied with ribbons, and the cornice was exuberantly scalloped. The bed hangings were a yellow cream color, with blue-and-yellow fringe. At the foot of the bed was a George III mahogany sofa in Prussian blue silk. English mahogany dumbwaiters piled with books were given pride of place by the fireplace. A Chinese Chippendale screen in the corner had vivid yellow panels. The oval rug is most likely by Marion Dorn.

RIGHT AND BELOW The grandest of the three Reed guest chambers was the Ivory Room, which took its name from the seven-and-a-half-foot-tall ivory-posted canopy beds. Frances found the posts in India and used them to create the beds, which were assembled in Monterey. The walls were covered in silver tea paper. Lighting was provided by branch-form Baguès.

OPPOSITE The bedroom's en suite bathroom was adorned with a hand-painted sepia-and-white Chinese wallpaper of flowering trees and birds. The inset dressing table had Queen Anne–style mirror panels; next to it is a French slipper chair in an absorbent terry fabric. The green-and-white marble floor matched the walls inside the tub. A beaded Baguès light fixture is overhead.

CLOCKWISE FROM ABOVE The tennis house was built in 1929, while the main house was in the planning stages. The Georgian-style structure included a gathering room with seating and dining areas and several guest bedrooms. The tennis court was sunken, with a spectator gallery off the gathering room. Mrs. Reed's daughter, Mary, was an ardent tennis player, and would often use the court.

The gathering room had bleached pine paneling, establishing a neutral backdrop for furnishings upholstered in shades of brown and taupe. For the dining area, a Flemish trestle table, Chippendale-style

dining chairs, and a Welsh shelving unit—all in pickled wood—display stoneware and pottery. The walls of the ladies' dressing room are made of Flexwood, a thin veneer glued to cloth. One of the room's angled corner cabinets can be seen behind the chaise. The chaise longue covered in raw silk was set next to a parchment table with pagoda edges and a white plaster lamp, both designed by Frank. A pale rug with a delicate flower design covers the floor. A guest, circa 1935, by the fireplace seating area.

Mr. & Mrs. Charles Jackson, Jr.

MONTECITO, CALIFORNIA · 1932

IN 2014, RANCHO SAN CARLOS, the 237-acre Charles Jackson, Jr. estate in Montecito, came on the market for $125 million, a record price for the exclusive hillside residential community above Santa Barbara. Incredibly, the property had been owned by the same family since 1927 and never divided. Even more astonishingly, the 30,000-square-foot main house, with thirty rooms, including twelve bedrooms, had been preserved exactly as decorated in 1932.

According to the Jacksons' surviving son, who had limited information from his mother, Chicago decorator Cornelia Conger (1887–1973) is the only interior designer associated with the house. However, suggestions of a collaboration with Frances Elkins and David Adler are myriad as Conger was a great admirer of both. She told the *Chicago Tribune* in 1965 that Adler was "the greatest residential architect in the United States for years." And for the October 1971 issue of *House & Garden*, Conger wrote a tribute to Frances's decor in the Reed house, singling out the ivory guest bedroom as one of the "loveliest rooms." It is also known that in the 1940s, Conger worked with Frances and Adler on rooms in Mrs. Joseph Ryerson's Montecito house.

Indicators of Frances's contributions to the decor are noted as they apply to the images in this chapter. The most likely scenario is that Conger was the official decorator but that she enlisted Frances and Adler to work with her on certain rooms. •

LEFT TOP A number of people literate in design visited the house when it was for sale, or saw photos of the rooms in the listing, and concluded it had a strong Elkins and/or Adler atmosphere. Frances's grandson, David Boyd, believed Adler contributed to the design in terms of the wood paneling and floors.

LEFT BOTTOM The living room, with its Georgian waxed pine paneling, is evocative of the Elkins style. The cream fringed sofas resemble ones in the George Camerons' living room, a 1930 Elkins project. The mantel and overmantel of the central fireplace are nearly identical to those in the Charles Goodspeed apartment.

ABOVE The two lamp tables by the fireplace don't match but are the same height, a Frances Elkins signature indicating her hand in the room. Many fireplaces throughout the house look like Adler designs based on historic precedent, including this one.

OPPOSITE TOP The library with its quiet tones, including the superb way fabrics were chosen to harmonize with the stripped wood paneling and the floors, strongly suggests the work of Frances. Another telling clue is how the pair of leather wing chairs exactly match the leather wing chairs in Celia Tobin Clark's library, decorated about 1930. The brass chandelier and the wall sconces are exactly the type of lighting Frances would choose.

OPPOSITE BOTTOM The color and strié pattern of the fabric on the fireside chairs and its fringe match fabric with attached fringe in archival Elkins materials, although the Jackson fabric is slightly

heavier. The choice of the six equestrian reverse paintings under glass and their framing harkens to others in Elkins/Adler projects, including the entry hall in the William McCormick Blair house, which had inset Currier and Ives prints.

FOLLOWING The dining room design strongly suggests the style of Frances Elkins. The use of the brilliant turquoise on some of the George I-style walnut chairs with yellow on others not only ties into the blue tones in the adjoining hallway (blue curtains, wall lights with blue beads, blue and green glass displayed in a window) but also to the Jacksons' china. The turquoise is a bold counterbalance to the subdued tones in the walls. The grisaille wallpaper is confirmed as a Dufour design. The subtly toned Samarkand rug with its quiet turquoise and other subdued colors is the perfect finishing touch.

ABOVE In the pub, located down a secret passage in the basement of the house, the selection of furniture, and how symmetrically it is arranged, is well matched with the antique English paneling.

LEFT In the guest room, a painted French provincial-style green chair with a needlepoint leaf design pops against the French wallpaper.

OPPOSITE TOP Van Nest Polglase, Jr., son of the noted Hollywood art director, remarked upon seeing the daughter's bedroom, "The twin-bedded chamber: so like Frances Elkins's work." The eau de nil raw silk fabric on the curtains, the chaise longue, and the dressing table chair harmonize with the greens and blues in the wallpaper, with its carnation pattern, and with the bedcovers.

OPPOSITE BOTTOM The Jackson house was a tour de force in the use of wallpaper. This guest bedroom was papered in a late-18th-century French pattern, likely supplied by Nancy McClelland.

Mrs. Evelyn Marshall Field

SYOSSET, NEW YORK · 1933–1937

IN THE EARLY 1930S, Mrs. Evelyn Marshall Field hired David Adler to plan a summer house on Long Island, for herself and her three children. In 1925, Adler had designed a seven-story Manhattan home for Mrs. Field and her then-husband Marshall Field III, which they only occupied for a short time before divorcing in 1930. Mr. Field, the grandson of the founder of the department store Marshall Field and Company, was a banker and publisher. Mrs. Field was from a wealthy New York merchant family.

Easton, with its red-brick walls and white shutters and trim, was Georgian in style and inspired by 18th-century Virginia houses, in particular Stratford Hall. Construction was underway by 1934, and most of the decoration was finished by 1935. By that time, Frances, along with David, was also decorating Mrs. Field's New York City duplex apartment in the luxurious River House complex.

For her discerning and well-traveled East Coast client, Frances infused the main house interiors with a traditional English character, but with an Early American flavor in the smaller winter cottage. Frances repurposed many of Mrs. Field's own English antiques, but injected contemporary touches to achieve a perfect balance and something au courant. These elements included Frank furniture and Giacometti lamps, modernistic floors, clean-lined glass molding and mirrors, and a few of Frances's own chair designs. There were oriental accents as well. The stunning result was one of the best examples of Frances giving the traditional a modern twist. A close personal friend, Mrs. Field underlined her satisfaction with the decor in a June 1935 letter to Frances: "Dear Fan,. . .I have just come up after a very pleasant weekend in the country. I had the house full and everyone is wildly enthusiastic about it. *I can't tell you how much I love it!*" ·

OPPOSITE Frances created a balanced and spacious arrangement of furnishings with a simple color scheme of white, brown, and beige. The avant-garde was represented in alabaster Giacometti table lamps by the fireplace and the gilt-bronze floor lamp.

ABOVE Easton's portico was inspired by Thomas Jefferson's Monticello and is flanked by Toulouse-Lautrec drawings.

OPPOSITE A seating area in Mrs. Field's bedroom shows the intricately molded mantel and chimney breast in the Georgian style; brightly painted Staffordshire figures are displayed on white-painted brackets and scrolls. A Queen Anne wing chair is accompanied by a needlepoint footstool and a painted standing screen as well as a miniature Louis XVI–style chair. A blueprint of the fireplace is seen at right.

RIGHT The chic Adam-inspired dining room had sixteen stucco palm pilasters reaching to the ceiling and set above a plaster lattice-form dado. Frances would employ the palm form in many of her 1930s rooms and would continue to use Serge Roche's palm torchères well into the 1940s. The rounded corners gave the room more dimensional appeal, with the curving plaster gadroon cornices at the windows. Carved-shells are seen over the doors. Mrs. Field owned the George III pedestal table. The armchairs and side chairs were covered in white leather, with button-tufted leather side chairs in pale gray.

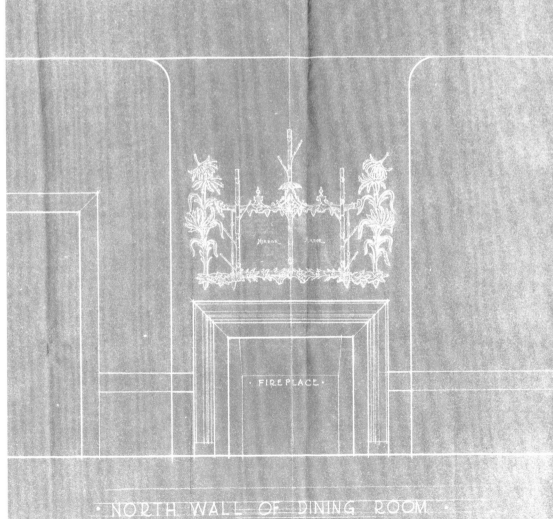

· NORTH WALL OF DINING ROOM ·
SCALE ¾" = 1'-0".

ABOVE CLOCKWISE FROM TOP LEFT In the white guest room with an antique mahogany English tester bed, Frances played with value contrast and pattern, including zebra rugs, white chenille quatrefoil bedspread, white walls, and a dark wood secretary.

The walls of the Chinese guest room and its adjoining bath were covered in an 18th-century Chinese hand-painted wallpaper from England. A white four-poster bed from Langhorne of London, possibly a Syrie Maugham design, was covered in almond green bourette.

For daughter Barbara's bedroom, an 18th-century document was the basis for the blue-and-white chintz employed on the bedspread, upholstery, walls, ruffled curtains, and dressing table.

The pattern was set against a cream white-painted four-poster bed, display cabinet, and pair of armchairs.

The guest bedroom repurposed for Mrs. Field's second husband, Diego Suarez, in 1937. The rug complements the bold black-and-white pattern of the Zenitherm floor. A Frank-inspired chaise longue and armchair designed by Frances lend masculine notes. The stepped design of the white fireplace embellished with black ornaments is repeated in the drawers atop the small desk.

OPPOSITE The walls and upholstery of Mrs. Field's bath/dressing room were a lily-of-the-valley chintz in cream, green, and blue. Frances and Adler placed the dressing room fireplace under a window. The fringed *cantonnière* was in green.

OPPOSITE An image by the great André Kertész shows the entry hall of the winter cottage. A primitive-style painted wall mural depicts the center block of Easton and is surrounded by elaborate floral designs. The Zenitherm floor was laid out in a pattern suggesting hooked rugs laid over tile. A chest, in burl wood, is flanked by two Hepplewhite chairs.

ABOVE The enclosed sun porch at Easton was decorated in shades of sand, white, black, and yellow. A Westminster sofa in a beige jacquard weave was accessorized with black-and-white embroidered throw pillows from the Royal School of Needlework. G.W. Scott, the English wicker company, made four deep-seated,

white-painted chairs covered in a tufted-yellow material. Tree-form bleached-oak standing lamps and matching side tables were in the same spirit as rectangular side tables with outlines of tree shapes, all designed by Frances. The four white-painted bridge chairs had backs carved to form eight open circles, nicknamed "loop chairs" by the author of *The Country Houses of David Adler*, Stephen Salny. The chairs are believed to be Frances's own design as well. The glazed floor tiles with diagonal black-and-white pinstripes are shown covered by an oval rug with a border outlined in black. Oliver Messel designed the white-plaster stag head with black antlers.

Mr. & Mrs. Harry Hunt

PEBBLE BEACH, CALIFORNIA · 1928–1934

JANE SELBY HUNT WAS the social arbiter of the Monterey Peninsula. As an intimate of Frances's, she and Frances were co-conspirators as the region's ne plus ultra of stylish hostesses.

Harry Hunt was not only a successful oil executive and cattle rancher but a noted sportsman. On her mother's side, Mrs. Hunt was related to the Athertons and the Macondrays, two prominent California families. Mr. Hunt played polo; Mrs. Hunt was an accomplished equestrian.

In 1928, Mrs. Hunt asked Frances to redecorate their two-story house designed by Spanish architect Clarence Tantau three years prior. The interiors that Frances inherited were furnished in the somewhat heavy-handed Spanish Colonial Revival style. Over the next few years, Frances gave the house her distinctive élan. She kept a few of the important pieces, but in the words of Harry Hunt Jr., Frances "lightened it up."

Frances created unpretentious interiors welcoming to guests and easygoing for the family. In most rooms, she used light colors set off by white walls, employing French provincial, English, and Spanish antiques as well as some modernist touches, including Serge Roche palm-leaf torchères.

Tantau was the most popular architect working at that time in Pebble Beach, and he was known in the 1920s for his Spanish-style houses. He and Frances would collaborate on more than twelve commissions, including the Hotel Del Monte in 1926 and the renovation of the James D. Zellerbach house in 1937. Tantau's interior spaces were in many ways a clean slate: smooth, unbeamed ceilings and plain stucco walls. In an April 1926 article, *Architect and Engineer* commented: "Another confirmed spiritual Spaniard is Mr. Tantau. He composes his forms with a simplicity that conveys distinction, and he achieves an execution delightfully appropriate to his design."

The twenty-acre Hunt estate included stables and a small polo field. The grounds were beautifully landscaped in the Italian style by the great garden designer and florist Isabella Worn. •

ABOVE Frances's simple approach to modern decoration is apparent in the main hall. The portrait is of Emma Lake Hunt, Mr. Hunt's mother.

OPPOSITE TOP The library's light tones rendered a mood of hushed elegance. Frances's signature use of a Han vase as a table lamp is evident.

OPPOSITE BOTTOM The bed hangings, cover, and upholstery in Mrs. Hunt's bedroom were white, blue, and green floral chintz. The tall revolving bookstand provides symmetry with the imposing French provincial secretary opposite.

Del Monte Tap Room

HOTEL DEL MONTE

MONTEREY, CALIFORNIA

1935–1939

WITH THE END OF PROHIBITION in 1933, the era of the drinking establishment began in earnest. Hotels and restaurants began designing them to attract women as well as men, rebranding them as cocktail lounges, cocktail bars, and tap rooms. Frances would decorate several in her career, including the cocktail lounge at the Barbizon-Plaza Hotel in 1934, the Tap Room at the Fort Ord Soldiers Club (it had the longest bar in California) in 1943, and the Surf Room at the Royal Hawaiian Hotel in 1947.

Hotel Del Monte, anxious to maintain its reputation as a glamorous center of international high society, installed two drinking rooms in the mid-1930s, one on the lobby level and the Tap Room in the basement. San Francisco architect Timothy Pflueger collaborated with Frances to plan the streamlined modern interior architecture, lighting, and seating. Painters Paul Whitman and his mentor Armin Hansen, noted members of the Carmel-by-the-Sea art colony, created the *In Celebration of Life* mural that included vivid, fantastical depictions of frivolous merrymaking—scenes of flying pigs, walruses, nudes, playing cards, and lots of drinking motifs—as well as sporting and hunting scenes. The pale upholstery in leather (or vinyl) was a neutral backdrop for the artwork's brilliant colors, with columns covered in mirror reflecting the room.

The racy sections of the mural received the most comments. In a 1939 feature, *The Seattle Sunday Times* called the artwork "the finest examples of humorous murals in America," with the writer C.B. Blethen stating, "No words can describe the beauty of the coloring nor the craftsmanship of these murals." •

OPPOSITE AND LEFT The Tap Room was renovated a few years after it opened, with another section of mural replacing mirrors behind a newly added bar. The images here show both versions and two small pieces of the colorful mural.

Mr. & Mrs. Leslie Wheeler

LAKE FOREST, ILLINOIS

1934–1935

THE LESLIE WHEELER HOUSE, Adler's last important design in the Georgian style, is one of his masterworks. Noted for its exquisite proportions, oriental detailing, and comfortable scale, the Elkins-decorated home was a sensation upon its completion in 1935. *Chicago Daily Tribune* writer Cousin Eve called it "absolutely ravishing" in her society column. "Rumors of the dashingness of this house have been abroad for months, and one can say that it is the most friendly and exciting house one has seen, perhaps ever."

Mr. Wheeler's family fortune derived from pig iron, while Pat Wheeler (née Rhoda Violet Patten) was the niece of "Wheat King" speculator James A. Patten, who at one time controlled the wheat, corn, oat, and cotton markets.

Frances and David bestowed upon the Wheeler interiors what *House & Garden* in 1938 called an "elegant eclecticism" tinged with a "Chinese Chippendale character." The mood was simplified traditional but also young and modern, with a refreshing color palette of light colors against white. •

RIGHT Full of lustrous surfaces, the expansive dining room combined a formal English disposition with traces of the Far East; it was a testament to Frances's ability to merge glamour with functionality. The flexible space also included a cozy breakfast bay and a seating area to gather by the fire. The striking color scheme included white walls, mustard-gold curtains, and a glossy black-and-antique-white Zenitherm floor with a large center medallion beneath a highly polished antique pedestal table. What *House & Garden* called the "classical severity" of the room was "lightened" with ornate plasterwork over the breakfast bay, carved pagoda pelmets at the windows, stucco swags around two prominent paintings, and slipcovered white damask sofas facing a bearskin rug at the fireplace.

OPPOSITE Decorated in blues and whites, the living room had marvelous contrasts of pattern and texture. Three blue-and-cream fretwork rugs echo the parquetry floor. The seating area featured a sofa and two Howard-style chairs upholstered in a Ming blue linen with white brush fringe. The bridge chairs, or "Elkins loop chairs," were made to Frances's design by Myron Oliver's workshop in Monterey.

ABOVE The library is the most recognized room. "David Adler considered this. . . to be the most beautiful room he had ever planned," wrote Pamela J. Wilson in *Traditional Home* in 1996. Four Queen Anne–inspired projecting bookcases divided the room into two balanced spaces.

ABOVE The walls of Mrs. Wheeler's bedroom were decorated in a Swedish green-and-white linen. The bed, chaise longue with adjustable back, and loveseat were upholstered in a quilted green-on-cream chintz with a swirling feather pattern. The carved mantel was painted white. The desk from Harrod's with crackled off-white finish and green leather top was paired with a Syrie Maugham-designed desk chair. Serge Roche made the two contemporary mirrors. The simple curtains were off-white. Three dark wood chests throughout the room added contrast.

CLOCKWISE FROM TOP LEFT This guest room had a stepped corner fireplace with inset mirror. In the sons' bedroom, Frances used wood-grain-patterned wallpaper set off by matching paneling. Another guest room featured two Paul Rodocanachi beds from Chanaux with red Fabrikoid nailhead trim. The custom commode with a faux-marble finish with elaborate eagle-form hardware was a big hit with Mrs. Wheeler. For Mr. Wheeler's bedroom, Frances used neutral Flexwood veneer walls. The sanded-oak bed was by Rodocanachi. The spare modernism was mixed with an antique serpentine-front chest and Georgian mirror.

Mr. & Mrs. Samuel Kahn

HILLSBOROUGH, CALIFORNIA · 1936

THE KAHNS FIRST hired Frances to redo the living room and library of their two-story home, Buckthorn, in 1936. In a December 1936 letter, Mr. Kahn praised the library: "I am delighted with the room and feel very grateful to Mrs. Elkins . . . for creating beauty without sacrificing comfort."

An electrical engineer, Mr. Kahn was president of San Francisco's Market Street Railway from 1927 to 1944. His wife, Rosalind (née Weissben), came from a family that had co-owned two California gold mines and founded a bank during the Gold Rush.

In 1959, the widowed Mrs. Kahn hired architects Charles Porter and Robert Steinwedell, who had been friends of Frances's and who had spent years working with Gardner Dailey, to design a smaller house a block away from Buckthorn.

The design of the new one-story residence, which Mrs. Kahn called her "little grass shack," was California style meets Italian midcentury modern. Mrs. Kahn wanted the Buckthorn library reinstalled in the new house, and plans were drawn to accommodate it. The only change was that instead of Flexwood veneer, the walls would be rift-sawn white oak.

The 12-foot-tall library, in both incarnations, was defined by the lack of articulated paneling, with no moldings or beveling. The arresting flat background modernized the room and made the beautiful carved fireplace—which Frances purchased in London in 1936 and mixed with a travertine surround—stand out.

The library was very much in keeping with Frances's rooms of that time and later. The room exhibited not only her appreciation of the modernist Paris interiors of Jean-Michel Frank, with their stripped oak or other spare paneling, but her deep understanding of classical English tradition and Asian art and antiques.

After Mrs. Kahn died in 1984, the library would have a third life when the mantel, wall sconces, furnishings, lamps, and art were integrated into the new living room of her daughter, Mrs. Irvin Gardner, also Frances's client. •

OPPOSITE The original fireside Howard chairs, Lawson sofa, wall sconces after Grinling Gibbons, pottery lamps with parchment shades, and the curtains and lambrequins in their original cream herringbone linen fabric were all integrated into the 1959 room. Art included Chinese Tang court figures on the mantel and on the wall near the fireplace.

ABOVE On the circa-1800 Sheraton mahogany double-pedestal desk rest a gold-leaf bust and a pottery horseback rider, both Chinese.

Mr. & Mrs. William K. Vanderbilt II

CENTERPOINT, NEW YORK · 1936

EAGLE'S NEST, THE SUMMER home of William K. Vanderbilt II, was built in stages over twenty-five years. The easternmost "Gold Coast" estate on Long Island, the house was a hybrid design of Spanish, Moorish, and medieval styles by the firm Warren and Wetmore. Frances is believed to have decorated rooms in the last addition, created in 1936, including the library, the breakfast gallery connecting the primary bedrooms, and Mrs. Vanderbilt's private quarters.

Frances's surviving project files do not contain documentation on the house, but Mrs. Vanderbilt's details are handwritten by Frances in her business address books, which do survive. A stylistic analysis of the 1936 Eagle's Nest rooms supports a firm attribution of the decoration to Frances. By the 1930s, Mr. Vanderbilt's daughter, Muriel Vanderbilt Phelps, owned a ranch in Carmel Valley, and the two women had many friends in common. Muriel may have introduced her father and stepmother to Frances.

Mr. Vanderbilt was the great-grandson of Cornelius Vanderbilt, whose fortune was built on shipping and railroads. A world record–holding race car driver, Vanderbilt was later known for his world travels on the *Alva*. Eagle's Nest was sited to allow the yacht to be moored nearby.

Vanderbilt married his second wife, Rosamund (née Lancaster) Warburton, in 1927. She was known for her sense of style and at one time was named one of the twenty best-dressed women in the world. A 1930s profile of Mrs. Vanderbilt in an unknown newspaper's ongoing "These Stylish Ladies" column saved in the Eagle's Nest archives wrote of her: "When it comes to her wardrobe, 'Fussy' clothes hold no lure for her—and her pearls are the RIGHT size, if you get what I mean. . ." But in terms of interior design, "Don't try to interest her in ultra-modern decorations." Mrs. Vanderbilt's refined sensibilities are said to have strongly influenced the look of Eagle's Nest from the late 1920s to early 1940s. •

OPPOSITE TOP TO BOTTOM The library displays Frances's particular mix of English, French, and Oriental elements. The carved

overmantel with broken pediment surrounds an 18th-century painting. Furnishings include French *Régence* chairs with floral needlepoint coverings, and Hepplewhite shield-back chairs. Mrs. Vanderbilt's luxe pink bedroom had Louis XV–style paneling and parquet de Versailles floors. The bed included a half-tester back panel with silk draperies and scalloped and fringed pelmet.

ABOVE The second-floor breakfast gallery connected Mrs. Vanderbilt's bedroom to her husband's chambers. Neoclassical bird-and-shell sconces complement the pickled-pine paneling. On antique English drop-leaf tables sit Jean-Michel Frank terracotta Chinese Pillow lamps with parchment shades.

Mr. & Mrs. Sol Wurtzel

BEL AIR, CALIFORNIA · 1933–1939

IN THE EARLY TO MID-1930S, Frances was asked by Mrs. Sol Wurtzel to assist her in decorating the Wurtzel mansion in Bel Air. The collaboration continued into the late 1930s.

Born in New York City, Sol Wurtzel was initially a successful producer for the Fox Film Company. When Fox merged with Darryl Zanuck's 20th Century to become 20th Century Fox, he was placed in charge of the newly minted studio's B-unit. Under Wurtzel, the unit made low-budget films that turned handsome profits. A native of Austria, Mrs. Wurtzel (née Marian Bodner) was known to speak several languages and to have many artistic interests. Like Frances, she summered in Venice. Her friends included Pablo Picasso and Salvador Dalí.

Architect Wallace Neff's inspiration for the house was Italian, and as he told the *Los Angeles Times* in 1931, "It follows the lines of the Florentine villas found on the hillsides near Florence, Italy." Neff's design is also said to have been influenced by the Villa Giulia in Rome.

The rooms Frances had the most hand in decorating reflect her sense of nuance, drama, and theater, together with 1930s Hollywood glamour. Her refined alchemy is especially captured in the opulent dining room, with its seamless combination of diverse objects from five or six different periods. "My great-grandmother Marian, who came from a shtetl outside of Krakow, Poland, embraced her new status as Hollywood royalty. It is likely that Elkins accommodated that vision," noted Sharon Leib, the Wurtzels' great-granddaughter in a 2018 email exchange. The house achieved a "splendiferous theatricality" in the words of Kevin Starr in his 1991 book *Material Dreams: Southern California Through the 1920s*.

Frances would decorate two other Wallace Neff homes in Los Angeles—the Spanish Colonial Revival–style Jules Stein house in the Beverly Glen district (designed in 1926 for film producer and director Fred Niblo) in 1939, and the midcentury modern Harry Kunin house in Holmby Hills in 1949. •

OPPOSITE The Venetian-inspired living room was the most extravagantly decorated room in the house. Molded appliques and inset paintings ornamented the flat ceiling.

ABOVE The splendidly classical Louis XVI–style double-height entry hall with graceful wrought-iron railings showed Frances's gift for tailored restraint. The exuberant Murano chandelier was purchased in Venice. Based on family lore, the 19th-century French standing figures may also have been sourced in Venice.

RIGHT The romantic powder room has elongated painted trumeau mirror panels separated by bands of mirror and two benches covered in orange velvet. The glorious plush wool rug has radiating textural ribs, possibly by Marion Dorn. The charming dressing table was set with an exquisite collection of perfume bottles and tole lamps.

OPPOSITE In the dining room, Frances upholstered silk velvet walls in chartreuse, one of her favorite colors. A set of cream-painted Regency-style klismos chairs with cream raw-silk upholstery are contrasted with Louis XV caned fauteuils in a warm dark wood. Dramatic floor-to-ceiling French Rococo palm-frond mirrors are placed behind Italian Baroque-style parcel-gilt consoles supporting carved neoclassical putti candelabra. The cream silk curtains puddling on the polished floor are trimmed in 1930s Fortuny.

Mr. & Mrs. James D. Zellerbach

SAN FRANCISCO, CALIFORNIA · 1937

THE JAMES D. ZELLERBACH HOUSE was one of Frances's most sophisticated urban commissions, with a style that could be called dignified, sumptuous, exquisite, and understated all at once.

By 1938, Mr. Zellerbach was president of the Crown Zellerbach Paper Company, founded by his grandfather. In 1949, he was appointed director of the Marshall Plan in Italy, which provided economic help to war-torn European countries in the wake of the Second World War. In 1956 he was made U.S. ambassador to that nation. Mrs. Zellerbach (née Hana Fuld), the daughter of a Baltimore druggist, was known for her sense of fashion. When the Zellerbachs were packing to move to Rome for the ambassadorship, the *San Francisco Examiner* remarked that "[t]his handsome matron, noted for her beautifully coiffed white hair and impeccable taste in clothes, seems admirably suited to the task ahead." The high-profile couple were also admired for their entertaining, what the *Examiner* called "the Zellerbachs' brand of hospitality."

Their 12,000-square-foot residence, built in 1927 for Frank Fuller, Jr., was designed by San Francisco architect Arthur Brown, Jr., a 1901 graduate of the École des Beaux-Arts. The Zellerbachs bought the finely scaled Georgian-style red-brick house on the crest of Pacific Heights in 1936 and hired Frances to redecorate it.

She would collaborate on the interior remodeling with architects Clarence Tantau and her brother, David Adler. What resulted were splendid rooms gently blending the traditional and the modern. The most acclaimed interiors in the Zellerbach house were the bar and adjoining card room. Both of these more intimate spaces were paneled with bleached oak, modeled after interiors by Jean-Michel Frank. Color was used somewhat sparingly—in a palette of mostly creamy whites and beiges—but very effectively. •

OPPOSITE The hushed luxury of the gallery established a sense of occasion for the house. Fourteen palm pilasters cast by sculptor Angelo Andriole define the space. Emilio Terry designed the

palm-leaf console and matching mirror for Jean-Michel Frank. To achieve her ideal proportions, Frances had the ceiling lowered two feet and sealed off the transom windows over the doors.

ABOVE Glass doors in a Regency pattern open into the inner vestibule. The vibrantly colored 18th-century Chinese wallpaper is patterned with flowering trees, birds, and butterflies in greens, reds, whites, and grays. Queen Anne benches in pale blue-green leather and an intricately blue-patterned Persian rug rhyme with the wallpaper.

OPPOSITE TOP TO BOTTOM The cool-toned white-on-white living room is given contrast and warmth by mahogany antiques, armchairs in vermillion velvet, a black-and-gold chinoiserie mirror, and brown-and-black Karabagh rugs. Syrie Maugham supplied the dolphin-form tables.

ABOVE Pickled-oak paneling established the refined atmosphere for the dining room. Frances had a Georgian mahogany armchair and matching side chair from Schmitt Brothers copied in Myron Oliver's workshop to make a full set, in cream velvet. The brass-and-crystal chandelier is Maison Baguès. The Greek fretwork rug was by Frances T. Miller.

LEFT The card room's light wood makes for an inviting mood. Frances designed the Spider chairs and table, made in Myron Oliver's workshop. The creamy-gray leather was supplied by Stergis M. Stergis. Jean-Michel Frank designed the metal-and-glass gueridon tables. Giacometti made the shell sconces.

ABOVE Mrs. Zellerbach's bathroom was papered in a shimmering chinoiserie. Chromium doors and silver tiles were used for the bathtub. A Louis XV–style slipper chair was in an absorbent terry material.

The cork floor retained ambient warmth.

OPPOSITE, TOP A guest bedroom was designed around two canopy beds draped with fishnet and tassels. A white-painted Victorian sofa was given a fresh twist with plaid fabric. The red floral rug coordinates with the color scheme.

OPPOSITE, BOTTOM The master bedroom was a soothing palette of cream and green. Giacometti lamps provide a hint of modernism.

Mr. & Mrs. Samuel F. B. Morse

CARMEL VALLEY, CALIFORNIA · 1938

FRANCES'S SCHEMES AT RIVER RANCH, the summer refuge of her good friends the Samuel F.B. Morses, were yet another example of how she created decor appropriate to her clients' needs and the style of the architecture. At River Ranch, life out of doors meant riding, swimming, canoeing, and picnicking, so Frances selected simple yet attractive furnishings suited to an unpretentious country compound meant for relaxation. When interviewed in early 2018, the Morses' daughter, Mary Morse Shaw, said River Ranch provided "splendid isolation." Frances understood outright grandeur but also the need to escape from all that.

A native of Greater Boston, S.F.B. Morse ran the Del Monte Properties Company, which owned the Hotel Del Monte and the Del Monte Lodge. His wife, Relda (née Ford), a member of a pioneer California family, was the daughter of a state senator and attorney general.

In the 1920s, prominent members of the Monterey Peninsula society colony were buying ranch properties in Carmel Valley to build summer homes where they could escape the cool coastal fog or simply enjoy a less hectic existence in gorgeous surroundings. The Morses, whose primary residence was in Pebble Beach, were among those families.

Starting in 1926, W.O. Raguel, the Morses' architect, designed two side-by-side single-story structures, one with a living room, kitchen, and small bedroom; the other with three bedrooms. About 1938, a dining room was added to the main building, and the living room expanded into the former bedroom. In 1930, Kingsley Ruthven of *Home & Field* magazine, wrote: "The two-building summer retreat of Mr. S.F.B. Morse of Del Monte is, to my mind, the happiest illustration of simple construction in a district which, *au fond*, is mostly decorated with lordly ranches and imposing haciendas. It is so simple that few architects would think of designing it." Ruthven also noted that "the owner has rigorously held the interior and appurtenances to the same simple tempo."

In 1936 *San Francisco Examiner* society columnist Susan Smith praised the couple for their ongoing efforts

to preserve the "sublime" beauty of the region, adding that their "own hospitable residence is ever open to their friends. Not only in their Pebble Beach house, but also on their ranch in the Carmel Valley, they have established the tradition of open-hearted entertainment." ·

ABOVE Film stars William Powell and Jean Harlow frolic with the Morses' teenage daughter Mary (right) and her friend Katherine Elkins, Frances's daughter (second from left), circa 1935.

OPPOSITE The two original River Ranch buildings look today much as they did in the 1930s. The low-slung main building was painted white with red barn shutters. The canopied deck chairs date back to the 1930s and '40s.

RIGHT A small wet bar was installed when the living room was expanded in the 1930s. The colorful mural over the sink was by Francis and Gene McComas. The saddle was a gift to Mr. Morse while on a trip to Mexico in the 1920s. The star-pattern curtains were red.

BELOW The dining room, including the furniture and decorations, is unchanged from 1938, save for the window coverings. Family lore is that Mr. Morse brought back from the East Coast an antique brace comb-back Windsor armchair, and Frances had a complete set made.

OPPOSITE Informal and inviting, this guest bedroom was decorated with simple American country-style furniture: hobnail bedspreads on the colonial-style twin beds, a slant-top desk used as a dresser, a rag rug, and sheer dotted Priscilla curtains. Color schemes were green and white, and blue and white.

Yerba Buena Club

GOLDEN GATE INTERNATIONAL EXPOSITION

SAN FRANCISCO, CALIFORNIA · 1939

THE YERBA BUENA Club at the 1939 Golden Gate International Exposition was unquestionably Frances's most remarkable public commission. In the clubhouse's lounges, dining rooms, cocktail bars, reception areas, and outdoor terraces, she created a spectacular succession of moods and atmospheres, from neobaroque glamour to quiet understatement. Representing many influences and inspirations, the general effect was festive and uplifting; both the interiors and the architecture of the building received accolades in local and national media. The two-story clubhouse was a gathering spot for California clubwomen, including ladies of high society (who purchased memberships) as well as for prominent visitors. From the day it opened, the Yerba Buena Club was the most popular building on Treasure Island, the site of the exposition.

"The interiors of the club are planned to establish a mood of gayety and good cheer," Frances told the *San Francisco Chronicle* in November 1938, three months before the fair opened. "It will stimulate the desire to dress up and dine and to foregather there with friends as often as possible." Frances's plan to use clear color in abundance was also noted. She was successful. The *Spokane Spokesman-Review* later heralded the atmosphere as "resplendent with color and ablaze with tropical flowering plants" and the rooms "so chic, so colorful, and so comfortable." In the same vein, the *Pittsburgh Post-Gazette* applauded the "slathers of gorgeous color."

Architectural magazines also heaped praise. "Inside, the Club is a complete phantasy [sic], almost Surrealist in tone, a kind of dream interior in which rich blues, the sharpest possible reds, and black and white are the colors chiefly used, except in the dining room," wrote architect and historian Talbot Hamlin in the October 1938 issue of *Pencil Points* magazine. "It is perhaps decadent; its frankly baroque or even rococo notes are certainly in the opposite extreme from anything we usually call modern; yet the whole is as fresh as it could possibly be, gay, insouciant, almost the ideal place to have a cocktail—or several." •

ABOVE Top, the main entrance, with multiple tiered planters. Bottom, the dining terrace.

OPPOSITE TOP AND BOTTOM Frances used gold accents throughout the main halls, lobby, reception areas, and beyond. This gallery has a large silver-and-gold Louis XV commode and gilt-frame high-back settees in gold Fabricoid. The shimmering theme continued with gold-framed wall mirrors. Mounted antler heads afforded a Surrealist note. The floors were black-and-white linoleum. In the lobby, a silvered reception desk with gold Fabricoid chairs greeted visitors.

PREVIOUS LEFT The small red, white, and black waiting room off the lobby was decorated in the Victorian-style with a modernist inflection. In a Surrealist touch, the ruffled black-and-white plaid silk curtains are daintily held back by plaster hands by Giacometti for Jean-Michel Frank. Strongly influenced by Frank but tempered by Frances's sensibility, the men's lounge was decorated in grays and reds; she designed the upholstered seating as well as the game tables and chairs.

PREVIOUS RIGHT This private dining rooms typifies Frances's matchless approach, with the focus on textural contrast. Chairs were in a red fabric of banded chenille loops by textile designer Dorothy Liebes. The table and console bases, believed to be the work of Serge Roche, were carved plaster. The silver candelabra is likely a Sigvard Bernadotte design for Georg Jensen. The use of glass ornaments as the centerpiece is indicative of Frances's attention to detail.

LEFT AND BELOW This image of the main lounge on the second floor was painstakingly colorized by Victor Mascaro from an image in the Elkins family files. The 39-by-58-foot blue-and-white room was mostly inspired by the 1930s Paris residence of Frances's friend, art collector Carlos de Beistegui. Fourteen curved Victorian-style sofas in bright cobalt-blue sailcloth with white bullion fringe were paired with red-velvet tufted chairs fringed in black bullion. On the chimney breast is a dramatic double cascade of seashells and starfish coated in plaster flanking a tall shell-capped mirror. Giacometti sconces are visible on the left. The rug was pale blue and gray. A rare black-and-white image of the room.

ABOVE The club's most dramatic interior was the 39-by-85-foot main dining room (another image carefully colorized by Victor Mascaro). Reached through a curving silvered hall, the double-height room had a silvered ceiling with yellow velvet artfully arranged as curtains, wall drapery in great folds, and swags above the balcony. The blue-and-white-striped window shades matched the balcony wallpaper. The tables, on black linoleum, were covered in pale-pink tablecloths with salmon-colored pottery plates. Lighting was provided by plaster Giacometti bowls mounted on lemon-

yellow columns wrapped with spiraling garlands of plaster leaves.

ABOVE The curving spiral staircase, carpeted with a crimson runner, with a central pole of plastic balls emulating glass was one of the room's most celebrated components. Frances took her cue from the spiral in Carlos de Beistegui's penthouse. Of the room, Frances's friend and frequent collaborator architect Gardner Dailey remarked: "It was like being inside a ballerina's skirt."[8]

THE
1940s

In January 1940, Frances was almost certainly still shocked and grieving from the sudden loss of her mother the year before in France, just as Hitler advanced into the country.

ABOVE LEFT TOP Reading Room, Soldiers Club (Fort Ord, California), 1943. Frances created a subdued masculine ambience with amply proportioned brown leather sofas and club chairs of her design; floor lamps inspired by Jean-Michel Frank; sofa tables and coffee tables made locally by Myron Oliver; wrought-iron chandeliers; and loop-fringed brown curtains by Dorothy Liebes.

ABOVE LEFT BOTTOM Tap Room, Soldiers Club (Fort Ord, California), 1943. The 90-foot bar was the longest in California (a young Clint Eastwood served drinks there). Behind the bar, the *Nautical Mural*, also known as the "Moby Dick" mural, painted by Carleton Lehman.

ABOVE RIGHT Frances Elkins with Bill Palmer at Monterey's Fisherman's Wharf, circa 1943.

OPPOSITE Dancing room, Carmel USO (Carmel, California), 1942.

SHE STARTED THE DECADE immersed in many West Coast residential projects and some contract work, but after the United States entered the war, she would aid the war effort by decorating clubhouses and USO clubs for the armed forces—Fort Ord Soldier's Club, Carmel USO, and San Francisco American Women Voluntary Services (AWVS). She even designed the hostess uniforms for the Burlingame AWVS.

The postwar period of the late 1940s—as the world recovered from the emotional and physical toll of the Second World War—would put Frances once again on the leading edge of high style as on the West Coast. But while most of her best-known work in this decade was in California, she had clients in the East and would continue to service her clients in the Midwest.

California's newfound place in the world unleashed a surge of creative energy. The West Coast and its bevy of talented designers, architects, and artists increasingly helped set a standard for gracious and alluring living environments the rest of the country could emulate. The indoor/outdoor suburban lifestyle came to represent something fresh and liberated from the past, just as other

flavors of modernism and multiculturalism would now join the mix of good decoration. It was also during this time that Frances started buying and selling Mexican crafts and using Mexican pieces in her rooms, making several trips to Mexico when Europe was closed off. It is thought she may have helped decorate her brother's house in Mexico.

Frances's well-heeled residential clients would still seek the traditional refinement, originality, and grandeur she could so ably provide, but less fussy (with the use of nubby fabrics, heavy linens) and commingled with a new sense of spaciousness as the country drifted into another round of postwar prosperity. In this decade, the modernist framework would dominate the look of many of Frances's interiors, with antiques and traditional elements often added for balance and a pleasant link to the past.

While continuing to present the homes of the upper crust in New York City and the country homes of the Eastern and Midwestern elite on their pages, the better shelter magazines, like *House Beautiful* and *House & Garden*, after 1945 would begin to more frequently showcase the good life on the Pacific Coast, transmitting the notion that

the California dream should become the American dream. Frances's work would appear repeatedly in these magazines after the war, including being featured in several cover stories.

Frances's services were once again in high demand not only from residential clients but also from hotels, country clubs, and restaurants wanting a new look after the deprivations and drabness of the war years. Some of her most memorable public commissions were created during this time—Royal Hawaiian Hotel, Santa Anita Racetrack (even more elaborately redecorated by Frances in 1952), Stern Hall, and the US Flag Centennial in Monterey.

In the 1940s, Hollywood also began calling, garnering her high-profile commissions for movie studio titan David O. Selznick and legendary actor Edward G. Robinson. The frenetic pace of her postwar decorating also provided many opportunities for Frances to work with leading manufacturers. She would now channel some of her inexhaustible creativity into designing furniture, bedspreads, and fabrics for companies like Baker Furniture, Cabin Crafts Inc., and the Colonial Drapery Company. •

OPPOSITE CLOCKWISE FROM TOP LEFT Frances Elkins, pictured in one of her 1940s visits to Mexico. She's standing outside the Tillett fabric studio in Taxco. Dorothy Liebes likely took the image. The two sons of silk screen pioneer George Tillett had established a textile factory in Taxco, which by that time had become known as an artist's community. They became associated with the use of Mexican manta fabric and were friends with artist Diego Rivera, as was Frances. Frances at the Hotel Victoria in Taxco, in a photo taken by her brother, David Adler, in a photo taken by Frances at the Hotel Victoria. Dorothy Liebes is photographed next to Frances on the terrace of the Hotel Victoria.

ABOVE Mexican Decorative Arts and Crafts exhibit, San Francisco Museum of Art, 1948. Frances curated an exhibit of over 150 examples of Mexican furniture, richly colored woven fabrics and decorative objects for a two-month display. Most of the pieces, including her Rufino Tamayo and her three Diego Rivera paintings, were lent by Frances, along with many items from painters Gene McComas. Frances's involvement with the Mexican artists was noted in a museum press release: "Her personal touch in slight modifications of forms created by the craftsmen will be evident to all who are acquainted with her work . . . . Particularly interesting are simple carved chairs, benches and stools covered with sheets of tanned leather."

ABOVE Frances Elkins (at left), Lee Dix, her man Friday, and office manager/secretary Harriet Weill arriving at the Royal Hawaiian Hotel for last-minute preparations two weeks before the hotel's grand postwar reopening on February 1, 1947. Royal Hawaiian Hotel brochure, 1947. The spirited cursive script is still in use today.

OPPOSITE TOP AND BOTTOM Design in 49, the de Young Museum's celebration of California's centennial, featured rooms by 11 San Francisco decorators. Frances and Dorothy Liebes collaborated on a "luxury reception room" displaying Liebes fabrics in gilded sandblasted oak frames, curtains and blinds, and folding screens. The Gourmet Shop, Pine Inn (Carmel, California), 1941, perfectly exemplified Elkins's knack for using electric color in some of her public work.

Mr. & Mrs. Thomas Bunn

PEBBLE BEACH, CALIFORNIA · 1940

FRANCES CREATED WARMLY inviting schemes with a cosmopolitan sensibility for the Thomas Bunns, owners of a long and elegant two-story house. The Bunns were frequently convivial hosts to the sporting golf and tennis crowd, and the decor was perfectly suited to a home in a resort community.

The Bunns' home was designed in 1939 by architect Robert Stanton as an updated Monterey colonial in white-painted stucco with forest-green trim and a shingled roof. Located near the Del Monte Lodge, the house was spectacularly sited with views encompassing the Pebble Beach Golf Links fairways and the blue Pacific Ocean just beyond. Frances would collaborate with Stanton on at least three other commissions.

For the large living room, Frances chose a bold blue-and-white floral fabric for sofas and tub chairs, adding ruffled flounces as a festive touch. Covered in the same textile were black folding chairs that could be employed as extra seating for the Bunns' annual Bing Crosby golf tournament party and other occasions. Frances's dining room scheme was disarmingly playful and lent itself to formal entertaining in a charming atmosphere. She used colorful panels of winter squash, carrots, butterflies, and—appropriate to Mr. Bunn's enterprise—heads of lettuce.

Known as the "lettuce king," Thomas Bunn was a produce executive. With Takeo Yuki, his partner, he created the Salinas Valley Exchange. The firm grew lettuce in fertile regions of California and was one of the first companies to make lettuce available year-round. Bunn helped spur the popularity of eating iceberg lettuce salads. A native of Pasadena, Mrs. Bunn (née Jane Austin) enjoyed sports, including tennis, as well as the decorative arts. In the decade after Frances died, Mrs. Bunn would remarry to Trent Hooker and become a professional interior designer. She would eventually work for some of Frances's former clients, such as the Pine Inn and La Playa Inn of Carmel. •

OPPOSITE TOP LEFT The hallway leading from the entry hall to the living room featured wall art by Gene McComas. The family story goes that overimbibing party guests walking to and from the living room would sometimes bump into the planters. They were eventually removed (the planters, not the guests).

OPPOSITE TOP RIGHT An antique French hutch with perforated brass panels, sort of a Continental version of the American pie safe, was embellished with Dick Knox green-leaf salad plates and green Blenko drinking glasses.

OPPOSITE BOTTOM The den was Frances's fresh take on the man's den and paneled libraries, which were traditionally dark and somber. The limed-oak walls strike a bright and cheery note and act as a refreshing background for the furnishings.

ABOVE A circa-1948 family image shows Mrs. Bunn (curled up on the sofa at right) entertaining friends. It is the only known photograph of the living room.

Mrs. Claire Brown

SAN FRANCISCO, CALIFORNIA · 1940–1941

THE CHIC TOWN RESIDENCE of milliner Mrs. Claire Brown with its breathtaking views was a collaboration between Frances and architect Gardner Dailey and landscape architect Thomas Church. The three talents composed what photographer Fred Lyon called "the triumvirate." From the mid-1930s to early 1950s, they were often hired as a team by Frances's discerning Northern California clients when building or renovating their homes.

Brown, the widow of Michael Brown, sold her hats in a Post Street shop in fashionable Union Square. In 1940, she hired Dailey to remodel her circa-1900 shingled two-story flat on Telegraph Hill. Dailey's modernization added a penthouse level, making it into a spacious duplex. The penthouse contained the large living room, which the *San Francisco Examiner* called "an upper-level room used for large-scale entertaining" and a wide sundeck landscaped by Church. Two bedrooms, a sitting room, and the dining room were located on the floor below.

For the living room, Frances arranged two primary seating areas with furniture well-proportioned for the clean envelope of Dailey's architecture. The windowed area on the right included a Jean Michel Frank–inspired sofa designed by Frances with a striped-satin weave fabric. She would use the same model in the Ernest Gallos' Modesto living room and the William Paleys' Long Island library. Flanking the sofa, bold urn-shaped lamps finished in parcel-gilt sat on stripped-oak tables with cabriole legs ending in *pied-de-biche* feet. Such a juxtaposition of aristocratic and humble country finishes was typical of Frances.

Frances's decor drew continuing praise in the local press and was featured in *House & Garden* and *Architectural Forum*, which commented: "Furnishings throughout are a blend of modern and traditional, illustrating once more the effectiveness of rich period pieces against severely plain wall surfaces."

And in 1948, the *San Francisco Chronicle* noted: "Restrained elegance is the keynote in the decoration of the Claire Brown apartment." The previous year, the *Chronicle* summarized Brown's interiors as "antique furniture in a modern setting." •

ABOVE Frances, with her extensive knowledge of European and American gardens, may have worked closely with Church to plan the terrace. South-facing sliding doors provided access to the 10-by-40-foot deck. Frances likely selected the graceful wrought-iron furniture. For maximum comfort, walls at either end blocked the wind.

OPPOSITE TOP TO BOTTOM A Roger Sturtevant image captures the nighttime ambience of the living room, "considered one of the most distinguished in San Francisco," according to a 1947 feature in *Architectural Forum*. The room's balanced composition is evident even in a black-and-white photograph. Two Coromandel screens (one is partly visible far right) framed the approach. The continuous pelmet gives the room a crisp, tailored look. A wool rug covers the dark wood floors. In the tasteful dining room, iconic Louis XV chairs with leather seats are pulled up to a Serge Roche mirrored table. Against the wall are Régence chairs, with their distinctive arched cresting, in a dark velvet. A Roche wall console is ornamented with large seashells. The antique French wall sconces held lit candles.

David Adler

IN 1918, DAVID ADLER, then an up-and-coming Chicago architect, bought a humble 1864 farmhouse in Libertyville, Illinois, a northern suburb of Chicago about thirty miles away. He would share the home with his wife, Katherine (née Keith), until her death in 1930. Over three decades, Adler proceeded to enlarge and transform the house in a classically inspired manner, giving it a mixed Colonial Revival and French country character. In the largest expansion in 1941, Adler added a one-and-a-half-story wing that included a newly enlarged dining room paneled in pickled pine and an expansive living room divided into two sections separated by a colonnade with white marble Doric columns.

The new room's tall, coved ceiling and simple lines provided a perfect envelope for a striking statement melding the old and the new. Working with Adler, Frances gave the room value contrast and used an amalgamation of cultural references and period styles, from 18th century to modern. For example, three 18th-century George III mahogany library armchairs in brown leather are paired with a low, dark-leather Jean-Michel Frank table and white-plaster shell-form ceiling light, marbleized white baseboards, and a Moroccan rug set in a dark and light pattern on low-pile, cotton strié carpets. Equestrian prints in dark frames add more contrast. The modern sofa was slipcovered in a diamond-quilted glazed cotton fabric in a tan floral pattern, with the same material used to cover the pad and cushions on a window seat. The gilt wood figure of Buddha on a marble stand near the window is from the early 19th century An armless Queen Anne chair in a pale-colored leather was stationed nearby. A flower-filled Han Dynasty vase and a white plaster Giacometti wall sconce of a stag's head are also visible. •

LEFT Over the sofa is an imposing six-panel coromandel screen, probably 18th century, in dark brown, green, and tan that portrays a banquet.

Mr. & Mrs. Ernest Gallo

MODESTO, CALIFORNIA · 1941–1942

FOR THE ERNEST GALLOS, Frances demonstrated the possibilities of rendering cosmopolitan style and comfort in a suburban ranch home. Working with architects like Gardner Dailey, William Wurster, and Robert Stanton, Frances decorated a surprising number of California ranch houses and modernist country homes. Her ranch house decor ranged from the humble, rustic, and countrified to the very sophisticated. The Ernest Gallo house in Modesto was in the latter category.

Dailey designed the low-slung, tile-roofed Gallo residence with overhanging eaves in 1941. Thomas Church created the landscape plan for the property, situated in a large vineyard with a vista toward distant mountains. Ernest Gallo was just 32 years old and newly successful when the house was built in California's bountiful San Joaquin Valley agricultural region. He had started the E & J Gallo Winery with his brother, Julio Gallo, in 1933, and the company would become the largest winery in the United States. Ernest's wife, Amelia (née Franzia), then 31, had worked as company secretary at the beginning.

Bringing the outdoors in, Dailey designed glass walls to take advantage of views into the backyard garden. Frances was careful to produce a furniture arrangement that would not block the scenery. The living room had a welcoming ambience suggested by commodious upholstered furniture, restful color, and the sparing use of pattern. Much of the room's ambience was expressed through texture. The simple wall paneling washed in pale jade-green gave the room a serene background. The clean-lined fireplace is framed with bolection molding. At the windows, tan-colored split-bamboo curtains bound with white and orange ribbon could be closed to filter the bright sunlight.

The Jean-Michel Frank–influenced sofa and matching chair designed by Frances were upholstered in a durable strié tweed. A large club chair and the seats and backs of two wooden chairs were covered in Mille Fleur, a pattern depicting flowers, hounds and stags, and birds in green and beige. •

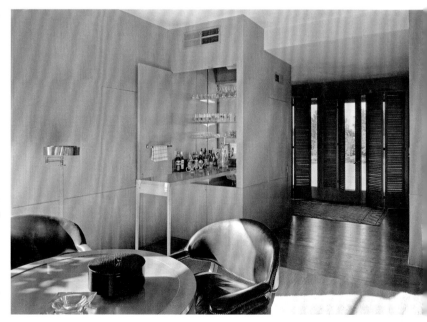

OPPOSITE Frances created an oasis of ease and luxury in the glass-walled living room.

ABOVE FROM TOP Mille Fleur fabric, now produced by Lee Jofa through Kravet. At the far end of the living room, a built-in bar (stocked with Gallo wines) emerges from a wall cabinet, a round table was surrounded by three low leather-covered chairs.

Stern Hall
Women's
Dormitory

UNIVERSITY
OF CALIFORNIA

BERKELEY, CALIFORNIA
1942

STERN HALL, THE FIRST WOMEN'S dormitory at the then-largest university in the world, was one of Frances's most original and imaginative public commissions. She had just returned from one of her trips to Mexico when she was hired to decorate the building, which would open in fall 1942. Her interior schemes were influenced by her love of Mexican furniture and colors—as well as her reverence for Jean-Michel Frank—with some Victorian and other elements. (Frances and Frank both had some fondness for the Victorian style of their childhood.)

When it first opened, the contemporary building, which initially housed ninety residents, was called a "modernistic queen" by the *San Francisco Chronicle* for its striking departure from the classical style of the Berkeley campus. The architects were Frances's frequent collaborator William Wurster, known for his simple modern buildings that strongly relate to the landscape, and the Beaux-Arts–trained Harvey Wiley Corbett. Stern Hall's benefactor was Mrs. Sigmund Stern, who wanted the dormitory to have a homey environment. Her daughter, Mrs. Walter Haas, an Elkins client, recommended that Frances be hired to handle the decoration, and Frances was thrilled at the opportunity. She provided her services at cost because, she told Mrs. Haas, "a lot of these girls come from small towns, where they don't know what good taste means, and I want them to learn." The early residents felt lucky to reside at Stern Hall, which they dubbed "Shangri-La."

Whether Frances prevailed upon Wurster to make the exterior as colorful as the interior is unknown, but the buildings were (and still are) brightly painted in ochre, terracotta, and blue, with yellow, red, and sand-toned detailing. Each wing was colored differently. The palette would suggest a Mexican or Southwest influence, or at least a feeling of California. The rooms have views of San Francisco Bay, the Berkeley Hills, and landscaped gardens. •

ABOVE In the drawing room, Frances produced an inspired composition, at once ruggedly informal and refined, marked by textural contrast and jolts of strong color.

FOLLOWING LEFT TOP The dining room had lacquered robin's-egg-blue chairs in a coral red, pink, and white wool. The dark-blue lacquered tables were covered in glass for easy cleaning. The floors were dark charcoal cement.

FOLLOWING LEFT BOTTOM In this library/lounge, Frances blended the crisp rectangular lines of the study table and chairs, the tailored curtains with box pelmet, and the Frank-inspired coffee table with upholstered chairs and sofa with pronounced ruffles, providing a feminine touch.

FOLLOWING RIGHT At that time, male visitors to Stern Hall were monitored, so this "beau parlor" was designed so that a chaperone could sit by the open door while couples conversed on the sofa.

Mr. & Mrs. Edward G. Robinson

BEVERLY HILLS, CALIFORNIA · 1941–1944

FOR FILM ACTOR AND ART COLLECTOR Edward G. Robinson and his wife, Gladys, Frances created inspired but subtle decor. While Frances was conjuring understated settings for the Robinsons' noted seventy-three-piece art collection to shine, she was also making rooms that would stand up on their own, with intriguing layers of complexity. The paintings and sculptures owned by the couple included works by Van Gogh, Cézanne, Monet, Gauguin, and Renoir. Describing the interiors conceived by "California's smartest decorator," *Chicago Tribune* columnist Thalia wrote in 1946: "The result is a masterpiece of charm and livability with the great pictures and sculpture an integral part of every room."

Robinson, whose career as a multifaceted screen player in more than one hundred films lasted from the silent era to 1973, was known as a sensitive and erudite man in real life. Gladys Lloyd Robinson, a onetime stage actress, was the daughter of sculptor Clement Cassell. She was a painter known for filling her canvases with color.

Architect Clarence J. Smale designed the Robinsons' English Revival–style house in 1931. A decade later, with the encouragement of Chicago architect and École des Beaux-Arts–trained designer Samuel Marx, the couple decided to remodel their home and to build a stand-alone art gallery next door. The goal was to have fresh and contemporary surroundings for the art collection, which they felt was cramped by the original gingerbread styling of the Smale house. Marx's remodel began sometime in 1941, and by fall of that year, Frances was working on the furnishing and decorations.

In 1929, Marx was one of the patrons of the shop Frances opened in Chicago's Drake Hotel (her records indicate he bought more than twelve items), and presumably the two were well acquainted. How directly Frances worked with Marx on the Robinson commission is not known. •

OPPOSITE AND FOLLOWING Shimmering silver-and-white Chinese wallpaper depicting exotic birds and flowering branches papered the dining room walls, with the cornices covered in matching silver paper. The deep mahogany Chippendale dining chairs covered in deep orange fabric were keyed to the frilly orange costume in *Jane Avril Dancing*, by Toulouse-Lautrec. Degas's *Little Dancer, Aged 14* is placed in the bowed window.

ABOVE A view of the large square downstairs hall. Playing with classical motifs, Marx designed mannerist Palladian broken-pediment door surrounds for the entrances. He designed the staircases with bowing balusters and a spiraling newel post.

OPPOSITE AND ABOVE The living room, with its shades of beige, was ideal for contemplation of the artwork. The seating areas were designed low to the ground, allowing for an easy flow and sense of spaciousness. Heavy woven fabrics by textile designer Dorothy Liebes were used on sofas and the large armchairs at the fireside. Frances injected contrast with the dark tones of 18th-century mahogany chairs and tables. As a rich accent, armchairs were upholstered in red. The ornately carved mantel, rumored to have been a gift from the Duke of Windsor to Wallis Simpson, gives pride of place to Renoir's *Girl with a Pink Feather, 1876*. The yellow sofa with gold pillows harmonizes with the grass in *View of Le Crotoy, from Upstream*, by Georges Seurat. Cézanne's *The Black Marble Clock*, a favorite of Mr. Robinson's, is above the piano; *Figure of a Woman (Before the Theater)*, by Berthe Morisot, hangs above the beige sofa.

RIGHT The skylit 2,000-square-foot art gallery had cork floors. Grooves inset in the walls allowed paintings to be rearranged easily. Shown are canvases by Rouault, Utrillo, Matisse, and Derain. Frances designed the long sofa, covering it in a glittering gold fabric by Dorothy Liebes.

OPPOSITE TOP The paneled library, with its quilted chintz-covered Howard chairs at the fireplace, was deeply comfortable. A portrait of Mrs. Robinson hangs above the clean-lined fireplace. In the foreground, Degas's bronze *Dancer* sits on a contemporary table.

OPPOSITE BOTTOM Frances's boldly modern loggia, with sofa and chairs in a rich carmine Dorothy Liebes fabric. The white walls were a dramatic background for Mr. Robinson's collection of primitive African carved-wood sculptures. Frances designed the ebony card tables and chairs.

RIGHT TOP Mrs. Robinson's dressing room was styled with chintz curtains, a white-painted dressing table and cabinets, and an English Regency-style bench.

RIGHT BOTTOM Frances made a very sophisticated statement in the primary bedroom with contrasting textures and the use of color. The fireplace surround is lapis lazuli, framed with pieces of old mirrored glass. The linen-covered tufted chair is in a color Frances called "hydrangea blue," like the flowers behind it.

Ransohoff's Department Store

FRANCES DECORATED TWO exclusive establishments in San Francisco's legendary Union Square retail district: Roos Brothers, from 1936 to 1939, and Ransohoff's, a women's department store, throughout the 1940s. It was a time when women shopping downtown dressed in their best finery, hats, and gloves, and when San Francisco had a reputation as a uniquely sophisticated city.

"Ingenuity plus a formula of elegance tempered with simple styling is the key to that well-groomed and highly fashionable look San Francisco women are famous for throughout the world. Smart and timely shopping helps too." Thus went the caption that accompanied a photo of two impeccably dressed women outside Ransohoff's in 1949's *Pay Dirt! San Francisco: The Romance of a Great City*, describing the sort of women who would shop at the store (and hire Frances as their decorator). In the 1930s and 1940s, a uniformed doorman would greet customers alighting from their vehicles. Roos Brothers had doormen liveried as 18th-century footmen.

The glamorous salons showcasing exclusive fashions at Ransohoff's were immortalized in the 1958 Alfred Hitchcock film, *Vertigo*, which depicted a gray salon in the French manner. The salons, decorated by Vail Kasper in 1948 after the store's Gardner Dailey renovation that year, were re-created on a studio soundstage for the film. According to a 2010 interview with James B. Ransohoff, Jr., who had held management positions in the family store starting in 1938, Frances had decorated various departments in the 1940s, including the high-end women's sections. •

CLOCKWISE FROM TOP LEFT The bridal salon, 1948, at once decidedly feminine and crisply contemporary, an Elkins signature. The millinery salon and main salesroom, 1941. A model admires one of the custom metal contemporary light fixtures affixed to mirrored columns in the main salesroom. The ground floor toward relocated millinery salon, 1948. It is unknown if Frances decorated the new millinery salon.

Mr. & Mrs. Lewis Lapham

SAN FRANCISCO, CALIFORNIA · 1942–1947

URBANE AND PARED DOWN to the elegant essentials, Frances's decor for the Lewis Lapham house reflected her ability to create beautiful environments for a client on a limited budget. The crisply proportioned and tall-ceilinged rooms created by architect Gardner Dailey gave her an orderly canvas on which to mix continental and Asian antiques with contemporary furniture. In the living room, which was widely photographed, Frances followed a warm and restrained color palette seasoned with bright accents.

In 1942, the Laphams, then in their early thirties, bought a modernist Pacific Heights house that Dailey had designed around 1937 for the original owner. The home's asymmetrical entrance facade was boxy and rectilinear, with the rear elevation on a steep hillside that incorporated a series of decks with views of San Francisco Bay. The *San Francisco Chronicle* in 1949 described the Lapham house as a "smart modern residence."

For Frances, styling the Lapham residence was largely a labor of love. "When we bought it, we didn't really have any money to decorate it the way we did," Mrs. Lapham recalled in a 1983 interview with writer Dupuy Warrick Reed. "And I said to Lewis, 'You know, unless I could have Frances decorate it, I don't want anybody.' And Frances by that time was a good friend.

"So I said to her, 'Frances, we bought a house designed by Gardner Dailey, and we're crazy about it. If I can't have you, and there's nothing in it for you, there's not a nickel in it. We haven't got any money at all.'"

"Frances replied, 'Don't be ridiculous. There's nothing I'd love better than to do it. And we'll do it as economically as possible.' And I knew it was going to be in great style and great taste if she did it. And she said, 'We buy nothing unless it has value, and if we can't afford it, we just get an ordinary wooden table and cover it with some interesting cloth.'" •

OPPOSITE Mrs. Lapham is shown on the deck off the living room, neatly lined with greenery in planter boxes.

ABOVE The entry hall's imposing double doors opened onto the living room. A white plaster palm tree torchère is combined with a white palm-form under a tall white mirror.

ABOVE AND OPPOSITE TOP The dignified living room fused Asian and European tastes. In 1949 *House & Garden* commented how "colors, textures, and periods blend easily." The room was arranged into two seating areas. A trim, tailored sofa and matching chair with square lines in a smooth off-white fabric are placed around a French provincial-style coffee table. An antique English rent table supports a gilded bean-jar lamp designed by Frances. The Laphams paid in installments for the $100 coromandel screen, which Frances found in New York. The screen's black and gold colors were repeated in the bolection-molded black-marble mantel, the gold table lamps, and gilt-bronze French andirons.

RIGHT AND OPPOSITE BOTTOM What Frances described as a "fine Regency chest" is embellished with old leather-bound books and a metal sculpture in the form of an anthurium plant. In the corner window, two loveseats with rounded arms and backs face each other over an old Chinese low table. Above the fireplace, an 18th-century ancestor scroll, which had belonged to David Adler, commands pride of place.

OPPOSITE, TOP
The dining room was decorated unpretentiously with a handsome group of antiques arranged before expansive east-facing windows. The highly polished table in burl wood reflects a cut-crystal candelabra and is surrounded by walnut Queen Anne chairs with damask-covered seats. An oak Welsh dresser holds a selection of decorative plates. Plain-colored curtains amplify the clean lines of the windowpanes. When reflecting back forty years, Mrs. Lapham said, "Frances, my God, she was really good. Things work and they were always comfortable. It was always a joy to do it because everything was the way you'd want it to look."

RIGHT AND OPPOSITE, BOTTOM The library on the home's top floor was furnished with blond-wood chairs and tables believed to be Heywood-Wakefield. The avant-garde ceiling light consisted of a strip of painted, corrugated metal with exposed, frosted bulbs in the valleys. Dorothy Liebes almost certainly created the nubby woven upholstery fabric on the chairs and the sofas facing a window.

Mr. & Mrs. Gardner Dailey

TELEGRAPH HILL

SAN FRANCISCO, CALIFORNIA · 1936–1945

IN 1936, AT THE MIDWAY POINT of her career, Frances began to work with architect Gardner Dailey, with whom she would collaborate on more than forty commissions. After practicing for about eight years, Dailey had shifted his focus in 1935 from designing traditional English, French, and Spanish manor houses to embracing modernism. Two of his early contemporary designs were his own narrow International Style duplex on San Francisco's Telegraph Hill and Whitney Warren Jr.'s clean-lined, more monumental duplex right next door.

For Mr. and Mrs. Gardner Dailey's apartment, as with all her residential work, Frances tailored her decor to the lifestyle of her clients and the contours of the interior architecture. The Daileys, who would divorce in 1946, were both highly cultivated people who had traveled widely. The debonair and well-dressed Gardner Dailey, who started out as a landscape architect, collected Asian antiques, Impressionist art, and exotic plants. His wife, Marjorie (née Dunne), was a lady of fashion, known for serving fine cuisine, and the daughter of a prominent San Francisco lawyer. Mrs. Dailey also had a large book collection that Frances made sure to accommodate, incorporating a capacious bookcase in the hall just outside the living room as well as providing spaces in other rooms for storage.

The four-story structure, which contained the Daileys' apartment on the top floors, had a separate downstairs unit. As with many of Dailey's late 1930s and 1940s designs, his own residence contained elements of the Streamline Moderne, an offshoot of Art Deco that emphasized aerodynamic shapes and sinuous forms. The curving staircase, suggesting an Art Deco ocean liner, rose four floors from the street-level vestibule and had white stair treads accented by slate-gray carpet and a smooth metal banister. The stair hall was painted a sharp shade of chartreuse, a favorite color of Frances's. •

ABOVE In 1945, Yousuf Karsh captured Dailey in the doorway to his living room.

OPPOSITE TOP TO BOTTOM The living room, with stunning 180-degree views of San Francisco. The window seating area consisted of a sofa, an 18th-century black Venetian chair, and a chair fashioned after a Venetian gondola chair, an Elkins signature. The elegant black marble fireplace is the focal point of the other conversation group comprised of two loveseats.

228

Mr. & Mrs. George L. Coleman, Jr.

PEBBLE BEACH, CALIFORNIA · 1946

THE GEORGE L. COLEMAN, JR. house was one of the most notable examples of Frances designing a single-story California house arranged for indoor and outdoor living, with its invitingly furnished lanai receiving much acclaim. Frances's scheme for what Gardner Dailey called the lanai was considered so distinguished it was featured in both *House Beautiful* (a cover shot by Julius Shulman) and *House & Garden* around the same time. The room, with its confident use of clear color, was also photographed by Philip Fein as part of a series of images of her California work that Frances submitted for consideration to *Town & Country*. Gardner Dailey designed the white-painted brick-and-wood-frame house, which consisted of a living/dining room, lanai, and two bedrooms, all with tall windows capturing abundant natural light.

The Oklahoma-born Colemans had been Frances's clients in 1936, when she decorated their baronial English-style mansion in Miami, Oklahoma, shortly after the couple visited Pebble Beach for the first time. Mr. Coleman was the heir to a multimillion-dollar oil fortune, with his own mining and oil interests, and an avid golf player. His wife, Elizabeth (née Fullerton), was the daughter of an attorney who rose to become a district judge.

Frances wanted to establish a simplicity for the indoor/outdoor plan, so she resorted to basic monochromatic schemes for the public rooms. Red and white for the lanai; blue, yellow, and white for the living room. In the October 1948 issue of *House & Garden*, Frances explained her strategy for the living room: "Except for a single French Provincial desk, which I originally sold them, the Colemans wanted to leave their Oklahoma house intact. So we were able to start almost from scratch at Pebble Beach, mixing styles with a free hand, which I like to do." The main bedroom is believed to have been decorated in green. This is based on a surviving pair of Elkins-designed bright malachite-green lacquered French-style chests of drawers offered for sale by a Los Angeles dealer for more than $50,000 in 2015. •

OPPOSITE The photo of the lanai by Fred Lyon, Jr. The main entrance to the house was to the left of the fireplace, hence the room has also been referred to as the "entrance loggia."

ABOVE In concocting what *House Beautiful* in 1949 called the "relaxing décor" for the lanai, where the Colemans loved to entertain, Frances designed the room around a central fireplace. She arranged large white-painted armchairs of her own design with vivid red sailcloth cushions by a round low table, white with black-marble top to form the primary seating group. Skirted tables were covered in cloths of red-and-white Tillett fabric trimmed with white bullion fringe. White "ice cream parlor" chairs employed more of the electric red on their seat cushions. Modern black pottery ashtrays and cigarette cups provided another black accent. The floor was glazed red brick.

ABOVE The high-ceilinged, blue-and-white living room, was an uncluttered canvas for Frances to create a crisp and comfortable contemporary statement. Two loveseats were covered in a midnight-blue-and-white German hand-blocked linen fabric and accented with yellow throw pillows. A Margaret Bruton terrazzo-top table anchored the grouping.

OPPOSITE Mrs. Coleman (left) confers with Frances in a photo by Fred Lyon for the October 1949 *House & Garden*. He recalled in a 2014 interview that the women, though friends, were nervous about being photographed, and he suggested they have a few drinks to relax before the picture-taking commenced.

United States Flag Centennial

MONTEREY, CALIFORNIA · 1946

ONE OF FRANCES'S most ambitious undertakings was the beautification of downtown Monterey for the United States Flag Centennial celebration, which took place from July 4–7, 1946. The celebration commemorated the 1846 raising of the U.S. flag in Monterey, the first territorial capital of California, and the annexation of seven Western states that had been under Mexican rule. Emceed by actor Robert Cummings, the events included a reenactment of Commodore John Drake Sloat's landing in the harbor, parades, dancing, and special appearances by Hollywood stars. More than 200,000 visitors were expected, and a local magazine called for a "face lifting." Something theatrical and memorable was called for.

Frances was selected to head the decorating committee tasked with creating the visual magic, her focus being the main thoroughfare, Alvarado Street. More than 100 storefronts were transformed with colorful paint using charming imagery symbolizing each business. Company names were stenciled in large print on walls or awnings in 19th-century vernacular typefaces, replacing neon signs. Frances came up with the concept for each facade: for a hardware store, a big can of paint, a hammer, and an axe above the entrance; for a seafood restaurant, giant fish, crabs, and lobsters on its walls; and for a grocery store, a hen laying eggs, stacks of fruit, and bunches of vegetables to cover the windows. Frances also painted the 2,300-foot-long expanse of Alvarado Street and its sidewalk gold, an astounding feat, accomplished with bronze powder donated by a residential client.

Frances also planned how the streets would be festooned. According to the *Santa Cruz Sentinel*, "Cypress trees, for which the Monterey peninsula is justly famous, . . . will line the streets, from which garlands of golden boughs will hang in graceful profusion."

The intended effect was that visitors would, as *What's Doing* wrote, "find themselves walking on streets of gold and viewing a veritable fairyland, transformed from the drab streets of a fishing port." •

ABOVE Frances's sketch for the Poppy cafe decoration and a photo of the final design once the neon sign had been removed.

OPPOSITE TOP Workers gilding Alvarado Street using pneumatic spray guns.

OPPOSITE BOTTOM Crowds thronging Alvarado Street and the garlands of boughs strung between light posts and cypress trees.

Royal Hawaiian Hotel

HONOLULU, HAWAII

1946–1947

THE INTERIOR DESIGN OF the Royal Hawaiian Hotel gave Frances her greatest opportunity to show the depth and breadth of her style in a commercial setting. "I tried to combine our Twentieth Century ease of living with the Polynesian atmosphere which is indigenous to the Islands," she was quoted as saying in a 1947 *Monterey Peninsula Herald* article about local craftspeople making tables, chests, lamps, and sculpture for the hotel. "'Most of the furnishings I used were done by Monterey artisans and they deserve high praise for their work.'"

The hotel, designed by the New York firm Warren & Wetmore in 1927, was given a postwar remodeling by Gardner Dailey and Frances, making it into what *Architectural Forum* in October 1947 called "a shrine of luxury and leisure." Dailey designed a new wing to replace the old dining room and a matching wing on the other side of the hotel for the Surf Room bar. Both the dining room and bar were designed to open up to the blue Pacific.

The main concourse in the hotel, the vast Oceanside Lobby as decorated by Frances, was given a simpler backdrop. She painted the ornate 1927 ceiling beams in off-white and the walls in the palest aquamarine, and added black terrazzo flooring. The combined effect of the sumptuous furniture, mostly her design, the tropical colors, and soft lighting created an exuberant sense of fantasy and welcoming cheer. Honolulu native Karen Schoenberg, who was an adolescent in the early 1950s, took dancing lessons at the Royal and remembers the impact of the lobby. "It was a very chi-chi hotel at that point. I was always in awe of the lobby. It was just gorgeous." •

RIGHT Lobby seating was covered in celadon green, pearl gray, pale blue, and in a few cases red, with coral accents on skirted tables. Gilded masks by sculptor Remo Scardigli supplied indirect lighting.

OPPOSITE AND ABOVE Two views of the lobby showing one of the two enormous magnesite chests. The color photo above shows fringed curving sofas, tufted chairs, and ottomans covered in celadon green, pearl grey, pale blue, and red, with coral accents on skirted tables.

FOLLOWING LEFT Facing the Pacific, the Surf Porch consisted of a lounge and a lanai. Frances designed the seating (here covered in a purple-blue sailcloth), the brass gueridon tables, and the low tables with black terrazzo tops trimmed in brass. Dorothy Liebes made the vividly colored bamboo blinds with raspberry-red yarns and gilt threads.

FOLLOWING RIGHT The diagonal plan of the new dining room created the best possible views of Diamond Head and the ocean. Frances chose Central American genisaro wood for the tables, which used Lauhala placemats handwoven in Pago Pago. Dorothy Liebes designed the woven teak blinds in green and gold.

RIGHT The powder room adjoining the women's lounge was paneled with wood washed in sea green, gray, and cream. Tony Duquette designed the large shell-encrusted silver urn filled with pearls and sea shells in the center of the settee.

Mr. & Mrs. Paul Winslow

PEBBLE BEACH, CALIFORNIA · 1949–1950

THE EIGHT-ROOM COLONIAL-STYLE home of Mr. and Mrs. Paul Winslow was the final collaboration of Frances and David Adler. It exemplified how the siblings could imbue even a modestly sized dwelling with good design, imagination, and beauty. "They have built and furnished one of the most charming houses in the State," wrote society columnist Susan Smith in the *San Francisco Examiner* in 1950.

Sometimes supreme works of decorative art can achieve the same aesthetic level as important works of art. The Winslow living room and dining room are as important in Frances's and David's career as the best of their grander commissions. The comfortable and informal atmosphere gave full rein to Frances's mastery of pattern, texture, and color.

"We just wanted a simple little country house, and this was what he evolved," Mrs. Winslow recalled about Adler's plan in a 1983 conversation with writer Dupuy Warrick Reed. Adler started to design the one-story, white-painted wooden house in 1948, and the design was mostly completed by September 1949, when the Winslows went to Chicago to meet with Adler. They were waiting for him to arrive when they were told he had died in his sleep. The couple settled into the house in the first half of 1950.

Paul Winslow held an executive position in the Del Monte Properties Company after the Winslows made a permanent move to Monterey in the 1940s. Mrs. Winslow (née Ruth Anderson) was from a prominent Honolulu family. Her composer brother, R. Alexander Anderson, wrote the best-known Hawaiian Christmas song, "Mele Kalikimaka," recorded by Frances's friend Bing Crosby with the Andrews Sisters in 1950. Mrs. Winslow managed the Del Monte Properties Company and was an influential real estate broker who continued to work into her early nineties. After Mrs. Winslow found an ideal mountaintop site for Adler on which to build his retirement home near Monterey, he asked how he could repay her. She simply replied, "Design us a house." ·

ABOVE The small entrance hall was no doubt inspired by traditional homes in Hawaii. The louvered doors opened onto the living room; when closed, they allowed diffused light to enter when the solid exterior door was opened.

OPPOSITE The more than 11-foot-high living room, with its vaulted ceiling, comprised 40 percent of the small house. The millwork for moldings and doors was in Greek Revival style. A black walnut star, a dramatic Adler trademark, grounds the Monterey pine floor.

ABOVE The bedrooms of the childless Winslows were in a wing off the living room. Mrs. Winslow's sitting room, in Frances's words, showed the "use of Swiss-printed chintz as furniture covering, for curtains, and as wall covering on both walls, and built-in cabinets around the fireplace." Rug and fabric designer Marion Dorn made the contemporary textured rug with its crosshatch pattern.

OPPOSITE TOP A living room seating group by the bookshelves. Frances wrote in a slide description how the "[p]arquet floor divides room into two living areas—one for music, one for library use." Mrs. Winslow remembered how she and Frances decided on green and white ,"because my husband raised orchids and she said, 'You'll always have orchids in your house, and you love flowers.'"

OPPOSITE BOTTOM LEFT For the dining room, Frances used one strong color to create a successful composition. To envelop an antiques-filled room with such a zinging color was considered remarkable at the time. Mrs. Winslow remembered that Frances asked her, "Have you the courage to let me do you a red dining room?" She replied, "Yes, I have the courage to have you do anything because I admire everything you do."

OPPOSITE BOTTOM RIGHT A detail of the sturdy woven floral cotton used on the chairs.

Whitney Warren Jr.

SAN FRANCISCO, CALIFORNIA

1936–1952

IN THE MID-1930S, Gardner Dailey designed two side-by-side modernist houses on Telegraph Hill: a large three-story structure for Whitney Warren Jr. and Dailey's own narrow four-story residence. Warren's imposing duplex, shaped like a rectangular box, had large-view windows and an expansive drawing room.

Warren was considered one of the most refined men in San Francisco. A member of the distinguished East Coast family and the son of architect Whitney Warren Sr. of the firm Warren & Wetmore, he was a connoisseur of European antiques. He was also known as a gracious host and a supporter of San Francisco's opera and symphony. He spent much time in Europe to further his cultural interests and to socialize with friends.

The well-traveled Frances, with her deep knowledge of the European decorative arts and historic architecture, was the ideal match for Warren. His opulent hillside home would occupy her time from 1936 to 1952. Based on surviving project files, it is known that from the beginning that Frances was very involved in the decor in all the rooms.

Her grand yet comfortable schemes combined many disparate elements to create attractive and livable rooms that pleased her client and displayed his prized objects to their best advantage. And with her sense of color, Frances created tone poems gently relating colors in one room to the next.

When the Warren apartment was brand new, Susan Smith wrote in a 1936 society column in the *San Francisco Examiner*: "Like a stage setting in itself was his apartment, with its spacious rooms and lofty ceilings, its attractive furniture and hangings, a masterpiece of the architect-designer Gardner Dailey." •

LEFT An evening photo by Fred Lyon, taken in 1947, shows the coral-toned living room in its late-1940s version, with its rich blend of furniture.

OPPOSITE A corner of the tapestry-hung library, where Warren would often host artist and musician friends as well as opera- and symphony-goers at post-performance gatherings. Here, Old World decor mixes happily with the new.

ABOVE A monumental Florentine Renaissance doorway frames a view into the Great Hall.

RIGHT Three 1953 Slim Aarons photos of a party Warren hosted honoring actress Audrey Hepburn, then in the play *Gigi*. Top: Warren, in a tuxedo, chats with Nini Tobin Martin (left) and Mrs. Grover Magnin. Middle: Warren warmly welcomes Hepburn on a pale-blue sofa with bright-red throw. Bottom: Gardner Dailey lights Mrs. Magnin's cigarette as Dorothy Spreckels Munn looks at the camera.

Frances Elkins

SAN FRANCISCO,

CALIFORNIA · 1948

BY THE 1940S, FRANCES WAS renting a 900-square-foot, one-bedroom pied-à-terre on San Francisco's Nob Hill to accommodate her visits to the city. The location was convenient to her friends and collaborators, textile designer Dorothy Liebes and architect Gardner Dailey, who lived within walking distance. Her Edwardian-era apartment had a small kitchen and dining area, which suited her because she did not cook and preferred to dine out or to have seafood delivered from Swan's Oyster Depot. The Fairmont and Mark Hopkins hotels, with their dining rooms and cafes, were only two blocks away.

Well into her career, Frances was incorporating a lot of black and white into her rooms. For one thing, she enjoyed using bold Victorian-era black-and-white patterns as wallpapers or fabrics in her clients' bedrooms, hallways, and bathrooms. For her own bedroom in the small residence, she fearlessly employed a similar design in linen as a bedspread, mounted as a piece of art on the wall, and covering a well-cushioned armless chair trimmed in black bullion fringe.

In contrast, her white-painted living room was defined by a charming mix of old and new, humble and formal, with its cream-painted Elkins rope lamp after Giacometti, Jean-Michel Frank upholstered chairs, French antiques (including a small Louis XVI desk and lyre-back chair), and a small Chinese lacquer screen, an item she often incorporated in her schemes. The rest of the room had notes of vibrant color, as *Harper's Bazaar* noted in April 1949: "The little white salon is done up in many pinks, from shell to shocking" and noted that there were "always pink flowers." •

RIGHT The pale-gray fabric slipcovers on the sofa are paired with pale-pink silk throw pillows. An armless chair is in a trapunto-quilted fabric with tiny flowers. Frances acquired the tea cart from a Crémaillère 1900 restaurant in Paris.

ABOVE The bold-patterned bedroom. A white plaster Arc table lamp by Alberto Giacometti is by the bed. Another Elkins white-rope lamp, an antique black neoclassical iron stove, and a white rug complete the scheme.

RIGHT The building's exterior.

OPPOSITE The kitchen lacked natural light, so Frances gave it a sense of brightness with a dynamic white-and-gold-striped wallpaper and paint, cabinets, and appliances, all in white. Complementary gold-painted café chairs were coordinated with gold faucets. A black countertop and floor provided value contrast. Overhead, an Elkins limpet-shell ceiling light, after Giacometti. When he photographed the room, Fred Lyon remembered: "I peeked in the fridge. There were a few bottles of good champagne and that's it."

Mr. & Mrs. Edward Topham, Jr.

ATHERTON, CALIFORNIA · 1948

FOR MR. AND MRS. EDWARD Topham, Jr., Frances created modernistic interiors that were well-suited to Mrs. Topham's status as a fashion original who appreciated artistic innovation. Frances worked with architect William Wurster and landscape architect Thomas Church on yet another quintessential midcentury modern ranch-style, taking full advantage of the outdoors with its in-ground pool and surrounding garden. Wurster's low-slung architecture included vertical redwood-board siding, a flat overhanging roof, and white-painted fenestration. The Topham house exemplified what *Harper's Bazaar* summarized in February 1947 as the Wurster style, writing that he "has probably done more toward selling domestic modern architecture to conservatives than any other architect. Californians like his rambling unpretentious houses, his use of native woods, the easy, livable quality of his interiors."

Son of a San Francisco surgeon, Edward Topham, Jr. was an executive with United California Theaters (later United Artists), a chain of movie theaters founded by his father-in-law, Michael Naify. Mrs. Topham (née Georgette "Dodie" Naify) would later become world famous as a modish international society fixture after she married John Rosekrans. In a profile a year after her death in 2010, Elisa Lipsky-Karasz writing for *Harper's Bazaar* called Dodie Rosekrans the "supreme style arbiter" who "proved that fabulous fashion is eternal." During her time as Mrs. Topham, she was already renowned not only for her chic everyday attire but for her spirited sense of fantasy when appearing at costume balls. "Mrs. Edward Topham rating a round of applause for she looked like a heroine right out of the Arabian nights," wrote the *San Francisco Chronicle* in May 1950. "Their hooded cobra costumes won applause Saturday night," reported the *Chronicle* in an August 1940 photo caption about the Tophams' getup. In another item from February 1957 describing her appearance at a Mardi Gras event, the *Chronicle* wrote that she looked like "a potential queen in a white embroidered sheath." •

OPPOSITE TOP AND ABOVE Two views of the entry hall toward the living room. The color image is from a later date and shows Frances's revisions. Artist Margaret Bruton designed the abstract pattern of terrazzo pieces inset into the marble floor.

OPPOSITE BOTTOM The simple dining room had a large dose of Frances Elkins midcentury glamour.

ALL VIEWS The teak-paneled playroom with furniture designed by Frances was believed to be in the planning stages when she died in 1953; it was left to her last assistant, Nelle Currie, to install the room. The seven-foot marine bas-relief may have been the work of artist Jane Berlandina. The coffee table with inset marble top is one of Frances's most contemporary designs. The fireplace surround is green marble.

Gardner Dailey

NOB HILL

SAN FRANCISCO,
CALIFORNIA · 1949

BY THE LATE 1940S, Frances and Gardner Dailey were not only frequent collaborators but also "very, very good friends," according to their 1949 client, Mrs. Irvin Gardner, in a 2015 interview. The two talents shared a taste for the antique and the avant-garde in furniture and art, and they could both be described as classical modernists, though Frances was perhaps the more traditional of the two. Both served on boards of the San Francisco Museum of Art (now SFMOMA). After his 1946 divorce from Marjorie Dunne Dailey, the architect's San Francisco residence would be a one-bedroom apartment in The Brocklebank on Nob Hill, just two blocks from Frances's Pleasant Street apartment. About 1949, Frances was asked to decorate the unit where Dailey would live until his 1961 marriage to his secretary, Lucille Downey. Thus, the decor closely reflected Dailey's aesthetic sensibility—and Frances's sympathetic style—without the input of a wife.

At the crest of Nob Hill, The Brocklebank, built in 1926, was one of San Francisco's most prestigious prewar apartment buildings and was situated across the street from the Fairmont Hotel and near the Hotel Mark Hopkins, both of which Frances decorated. Described as having "the most beautiful and luxurious apartments west of New York" in 1926 advertisements, The Brocklebank exterior stood in as the residence for various film characters, most notably Kim Novak's Madeleine Elster in Hitchcock's *Vertigo* (1958).

Dailey's apartment perfectly suited a worldly, suave, art-savvy man-about-town, one who might be attending a cocktail party or dining out after hours at his favorite restaurant, Place Pigalle. Frances's decor anticipates the mature style of decorator Billy Baldwin and also has some of the rich flavor of Coco Chanel's Rue Cambon apartment. •

RIGHT The living room's imposing 19th-century coromandel screen is juxtaposed with trim, tailored contemporary sofas and matching chairs, possibly designed by Frances and Dailey.

OPPOSITE The view into the living room shows a carved rosewood 19th-century Ching Dynasty table, with bonsai maples trees in a square white planter. On the hardwood floor is a brown-wool Stardust rug with sparkling highlights of metallic threads.

ABOVE A wallpaper of gray squares with a linen-like texture provided a smart backdrop in the bedroom, which also served as a den or library. A daybed in ebonized wood is in a crimson-colored, diamond-quilted fabric, intriguingly patterned. Panels of a black-and-gold Chinese lacquer screen flank the daybed.

LEFT This living room detail shows Frances's facility for arranging pieces of varying scale in a cohesive manner. The curves in one of the gondola chairs balance the square forms of the armchair and 19th-century Chinese cabinet.

Dr. & Mrs. Irvin Gardner

HILLSBOROUGH, CALIFORNIA · 1949

THE DR. AND MRS. IRVIN GARDNER house was a fine post-war example of a very contemporary type of California ranch house as interpreted by architect Gardner Dailey. Dailey gave the Gardner home clean rectangular lines, a flat roof, and the sort of refined fenestration the architect was known for. The gray-painted stucco exterior had white trim, with the lanai wing (pictured here) formed of vertical board-and-batten painted white. The house spread out over three wings, two of which framed a backyard with lawn, and later a pool, landscaped by Thomas Church. Frances's innovative use of terrace furniture for the lanai, a combination living/dining room that made up one of the home's wings, was particularly notable.

Dr. Gardner was a prominent obstetrician (he delivered Frances's grandchildren) and also president of the Baywood Oil Company. Mrs. Gardner (née Barbara Kahn) was the daughter of the Samuel Kahns, clients of Frances in the mid-1930s.

The lanai served as the primary gathering spot for the Gardners and their three boys. A glass wall had two sliding sections that could be opened for easy access to the terrace. The lanai had what *House & Garden* in 1957 called an "informal air," with its exposed beams, outdoor furniture and fabrics, and brick floor, which extended to the terrace. The furniture layout facilitated an easy flow through areas for lounging, dining, and card playing.

"We were the youngest clients they ever had, with the most limited budget," Mrs. Gardner recalled in a 2015 interview. They had nothing in the way of suitable furnishings but had received fine china as a wedding gift. Frances was not impressed. Mrs. Gardner recounted: "She said, 'You can't sit on a Lowestoft plate!' At that age, we were still sitting around on the floor. We didn't have enough chairs." Frances not only selected seating for the rooms, but she also gave Mrs. Gardner valuable advice: "She told me how we could entertain. She said, 'spaghetti and French bread and a lot of red wine.'" Mrs. Gardner was very happy with the results Frances and Dailey produced. "They did a wonderful job. They'd just treat us like children. In a sense we were." •

ALL VIEWS For the lanai, strong value contrast was employed to add some formality. The sofa with black upholstery had white bullion fringe, accessorized with fringed white throw pillows. The brick floors were dark gray. Black tole table lamps with white parchment shades sat on raised white shelf tables. The walls and ceiling were painted off-white. One of a pair of Elkins-designed floor lamps outlined in spiraling metal adds another white note.

Mr. & Mrs. Walter Haas

SAN FRANCISCO,
CALIFORNIA · 1949

THE WALTER HAASES had been clients of Frances's since the 1930s, when she decorated their Atherton country estate designed by Gardner Dailey in 1927. When they purchased the 5,000-square-foot prewar penthouse they had been renting in San Francisco, Frances was enlisted to handle the renovation, a job that involved modifying the interior architecture. Frances was able to incorporate many pieces Mrs. Haas already owned, including tapestry-covered Louis XVI fauteuils. The couple's art collection, which included Matisse's vividly colored *La Femme au chapeau* (1905), was integrated into the decor.

As president and chairman of Levi Strauss starting in 1919, Walter Haas built the firm into the world's largest clothing manufacturer. (The company had been founded by Mrs. Haas's great-uncle.) His leadership of the firm for more than fifty years would revolutionize fashion, elevating blue jeans from denim work clothes to the preferred attire of America's youth. A major arts patron and civic leader, Mrs. Haas (née Elise Stern) was the first woman president of both the San Francisco Museum of Modern Art and Mount Zion Hospital. Frances would go on to decorate the museum's member quarters and the hospital's reception areas.

A major booster of Frances's, Mrs. Haas introduced Frances to Rosalie Stern, her mother, which resulted in her decorating not only Mrs. Stern's house but Stern Hall women's dormitory. And Mrs. Haas's daughter, Rhoda Goldman, would be one of Frances's last residential clients.

In oral history interviews from 1979, Mrs. Haas spoke of her city residence, with "its unbelievable view. . . . It is a beautiful background for our works of art. In my opinion, Frances had the most perfect taste of anyone, and without compromising what she liked, she managed to adapt to her clients' tastes." •

RIGHT Frances gave the living room, with its spectacular outlook toward Russian Hill and San Francisco Bay, an understated refinement by choosing pale gray for the walls and the matching curtains.

THE
1950s

The early years of the 1950s would represent the final chapter of Frances Elkins's life and career. In that narrow window of time, Frances would complete several residential and commercial projects with her superb discrimination, which by themselves would be a remarkable oeuvre in any interior designer's career.

OPPOSITE Les Chasses de Compiègne (The Hunts of Compiègne) wallpaper used in the bar area of the Directors' Room, Los Angeles Turf Club, Santa Anita Park (Arcadia, California), 1952.

ABOVE Members Room, San Francisco Museum of Art, 1952.

OPPOSITE ABOVE Dining room, Bernard Ford residence (Hillsborough, California), 1953. One of Frances's last residential commissions, the modernist Ford house designed by Gardner Dailey in a Japanese-style featured several signature Elkins touches. The room, all of a piece in polished wood, featured a Queen Anne table and chairs and an old tapestry depicting a pastoral scene. Antique English sideboard, an ornate giltwood mirror, and streamlined metal uplights were also part of the ensemble.

OPPOSITE BOTTOM Playroom, Richard Zellerbach residence (Menlo Park, California), 1951. Frances's masterful color sense was in full display in the midcentury modern playroom. A clown painting is the key to the room's color scheme and harlequin floor. The wood-paneled walls are washed in soft gray to match the brick fireplace, combined with pale gray curtains in a matching box pelmet.

FRANCES WOULD MOST LIKELY have also started the 1950s still in mourning for her brother, David, who had died in September 1949. After his death, she worked to preserve Adler's house in Libertyville, Illinois, and turn it into a cultural center. In November 1999, the house was nominated to the National Register of Historic Places and functions as an arts center today.

The houses Frances decorated in the 1950s covered a wide gamut of styles, incorporating her customary eclecticism and local as well as international sources and inspirations.

From the dramatic black, white, and red interiors in the restrained midcentury modern Richard Goldman house to the grand formality of the antiques-filled Sidney Ehrman mansion to the simple down-home American country flavor of the McKinley Bissinger weekend house, Frances's 1950s residential portfolio was impressive. The Albert Schlesinger house, designed to accommodate Mrs. Schlesinger's love of dressed-up nighttime entertaining, may have been her most arrestingly innovative residential decor during these years. Across the San Francisco Bay, the Japanese-style home of Mr. and Mrs. Stewart Hopps, designed for cocktail parties that overflowed onto its long

series of decks with spectacular views, would give Frances free rein to mix French provincial antiques with her spin on Japanese modern, a rare feat in American decorating.

Some of Frances's outstanding 1950s commercial work included what a 1955 *Sports Illustrated* story would headline as the "Trackside Luxury"[9] of the Los Angeles Turf Club at Santa Anita Park, which Frances redecorated for the second time in 1952, and the clean-lined "tiki" glamour she concocted for Gardner Dailey's International-style SurfRider Hotel, her second project for the Matson company in Honolulu.

All of her 1950s creations exemplified Frances's continuing mastery of symmetry and scale, her ability to create pleasing contrasts of color and texture, and her love of mixing old and new, grand and humbler, and the bold with the understated.

In 1952, *Who's Who of American Women* mailed Frances a questionnaire, informing her they wanted to include her biography in their 1954 edition. The form, which asks her to describe her schooling, was apparently never submitted. The blank questionnaire was found in her effects when she died in August 1953. Had Frances lived and had her biography appeared in the 1954 *Who's Who*, specifics about whether or not she pursued actual courses in interior design might have emerged. But there is something telling in the *What's Doing* profile about Frances's

relationship to David Adler, which notes that "much of her perfectionism in her art stems from a desire to please his exacting standards."[10] •

ABOVE LEFT Elizabeth "Beegle" Duquette, the artist wife of designer Tony Duquette, visits Frances in her Fisherman's Wharf office, circa 1952.

ABOVE RIGHT Members Room, San Francisco Museum of Art, 1952. As a backdrop, walls are painted a pale gray. Frances used the most up-to-the-minute materials: black-and-gold coin-studded low tables in phenolic resin by Monterey artist and former San Francisco art dealer Guthrie Courvoisier, along with his six-panel gold-and-black plastic screen.

OPPOSITE Living room, Stewart Hopps residence (Belvedere, California), 1952. In a Japanese-modern house designed by Robert Stanton, cantilevered over a steep cliff on San Francisco Bay, Frances created rooms inspired by Asian and French provincial styles. The palette of teals and dark oranges is likely keyed to the robe of an antique carved Quan Yin statute in the room. Open-armed teal sofas were placed opposite a modern cocktail table with legs from a 19th-century Japanese altar table.

Mr. & Mrs. Morgan Gunst

SAN FRANCISCO, CALIFORNIA · 1948–1953

COLLABORATING WITH ARCHITECT William Wurster and associate Donn Emmons, Frances gave the 33-year-old Pacific Heights house of Mr. and Mrs. Morgan Gunst an innovative makeover in 1948. The remodeled rooms were simpler, more spacious, and, as Mrs. Gunst told the *San Francisco Chronicle* in a 1950 home feature, "more livable." Gone was the dark and weighty paneling and molding in the living room, dining room, and library. Frances instilled a modern spirit in the house with contemporary furnishings and lamps, Dorothy Liebes handwoven textiles, and appealing color combinations. But in her usual fashion, Frances successfully integrated traditional elements such as Georgian, Louis XVI, French provincial and Chinese antiques, and old Chinese ceramics. The result was what the *Chronicle* called "an old house made new."

Son of a millionaire cigar company founder, Morgan Gunst was vice-president of the Bank of America, chairman of San Francisco's Redevelopment Agency, and active in city planning. He was known for his collection of rare books, which he displayed at the 1939 Golden Gate International Exposition. Mrs. Gunst (née Aline Dreyfus) was active in the California School of Fine Arts and a friend of local artists, including photographer Imogen Cunningham.

The *Chronicle* speculated that Frances keyed the library decor to Mrs. Gunst's blonde hair, olive skin, and blue-green eyes. Various handwoven Liebes textiles are used throughout the room. The color palette included rust, tangerine, apricot, blue, and lavender. Fireside and window seating is upholstered in beige. A sofa in the foreground and two antique fauteuils have lavender coverings. Throw pillows in plain and sparkling striped Liebes textiles are strewn on the sofas. Frances designed the square modern coffee table, which she combined with a variety of antique Chinese tables, some lacquered black. A Giacometti gilt-bronze Pomme De Pin sculptural floor lamp harmonizes with decorative gold bowls and ashtrays. The absence of wall art is not uncommon in Frances's work, likely influenced by Jean-Michel Frank, who preferred that walls be left blank. •

ABOVE FROM TOP Bold blue-and-cream botanical chintz in Mrs. Gunst's office. For the main bedroom, the curtains and sofa were a pink damask, and the beds were handwoven Liebes fabric.

OPPOSITE The quiet backdrop for the library was drift-oak walls, with matching Dorothy Liebes fabrics at the windows.

Frances Elkins

CARMEL VALLEY, CALIFORNIA · 1928–1953

IN 1928, FRANCES AND DAVID ADLER bought a 130-acre ranch in Carmel Valley. Adler designed for Frances a simple wood-framed home she could use as a summer and weekend retreat from the cool Monterey coastal climate. Adler's initial drawings show a compact structure, which was almost certainly expanded over time.

The living room and reception room of this secluded getaway are shown in these circa 1950 Tony Duquette slides. Frances brought her sophistication with her to this rustic setting, mixing styles and periods as she often did. The decoration allowed Frances to use one of her favorite color combinations: blue and yellow, with the yellow represented in the panels of the warm knotty pine walls.

In the entry area, Frances painted the unpaneled walls in teal and aqua, with teal also used for the fabric on the Swedish settee and matching chair. Marbleized painted panels are seen on the Dutch door.

A view of the living room with its pitched ceiling depicts the contrast of the rustic wood with the luxurious tufted blue satin upholstery on the low-to-the-ground sofa and chair, possibly scaled to make the short-statured Frances look her best. A large early-19th-century continental family portrait, a white-painted sea nymph console table, and a coffee table with seashells under glass create an eclectic mix. The elegant furniture is very unexpected in a country cabin!

The cabinetry for the built-in bookcase in the living room shows more of the marbleized paint on the barnwood used for an under-cabinet, needlepoint-covered Regence chairs, a Louis XVI French chair with goldish silk brocade, and white-painted parcel gilt neoclassical armchairs upholstered in blue silk. Frances took late-19th-century wooden industrial fabric or wallpaper rollers and fashioned them into table lamps with pink silk lampshades. Beautiful leather-bound books, Chinese vases, and Spanish baroque altar figures are also part of the arrangement.

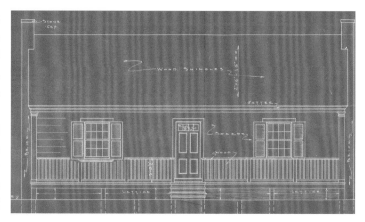

At the back of the living room was a piano (Frances likely continued to play), gilded Louis XVI chairs in chartreuse velvet, a coat of arms on the wall, a French cartel clock, and another view of the blue upholstery, needlepoint chairs, white-painted chair, and inventive table lamps, against dark hardwood floors. •

ABOVE David Adler's sketches for the Carmel Valley ranch house.

OPPOSITE Tony Duquette took these color photographs. Duquette's wife, "Beegle," is captured during the visit. The knotty pine panels give the rooms a warm, rustic feeling, but the furniture and accessories add Frances's signature sophistication.

Mr. & Mrs. Robert Wiel

SAN FRANCISCO, CALIFORNIA · 1950

EVEN LATE IN HER CAREER, Frances would give full sway to her love of French provincial furniture. The home of Mr. and Mrs. Robert Wiel, which was one of the seven commissions featured in the San Francisco Museum of Art's 1954 Elkins tribute tour, placed the fine French country furniture in its public rooms on centerstage. But as she was wont to do in so many of her commissions, Frances accessorized with a few Asian pieces (like the 18th-century Chinese lacquer screen in the living room) and modernist touches (for example, a spiral-form corkscrew floor lamp and a white plaster table lamp) to make the interiors feel as fresh as possible.

Mr. Wiel was president of Cypress-Abbey, a real estate firm, while his wife, Marjorie (née Loewe), was the stepdaughter of Louis Schwabacher, an executive with the Hotel St. Francis. Frances would decorate for other members of the Schwabacher family, as well as guest rooms and a cocktail lounge at the St. Francis. The Wiels were regular patrons of the San Francisco Opera and breeders of award-winning Kerry Blue terriers. Mrs. Wiel was named by *Life* magazine in 1947 as the best-dressed woman in San Francisco. •

OPPOSITE The living room, showing two of the three seating areas. Frances calls attention to the "curtain detail and section of fine coromandel screen . . . . Pale blue walls act as complementary background for fine French provincial wood pieces collected by Mrs. Wiel and Mrs. Elkins."

LEFT FROM TOP Frances wrote how the entrance hall showed "the use of hand-blocked wallpaper panels above dadoes," while the stairwell had "three panels framed as décor." The paper, black on white, depicts farm workers harvesting apples, possibly in California. The black-and-white floor, possibly linoleum or terrazzo, relates to the black-and-white stair runner. Frances gave the dining room her special verve with a bold hand-blocked red toile wallpaper.

Mr. & Mrs. Richard Goldman

SAN FRANCISCO, CALIFORNIA · 1952

A "STRIKINGLY MODERN HOME" is how the *Oakland Tribune* characterized the Goldman house and its decor in its February 17, 1954, wrap-up of the Frances Elkins tribute tour sponsored by the San Francisco Museum of Art. The project was an instance where Frances dialed up the value contrast to the maximum. Her schemes for the downstairs public rooms suited the contemporary architecture, and it was in that moment in Frances's career during which she used a lot of black, white, and red. In describing the five homes on the tribute tour, four of which dated from the late 1940s and early 1950s, the *Tribune* noted, "Each room contained at least one black or white accent—as though they were the decorator's signature."

Richard Goldman was the president of Goldman Insurance Services, an insurance brokerage firm he founded in 1949. Mrs. Goldman (née Rhoda Haas) was the daughter of Frances's clients Walter Haas and Elise Stern Haas, who through her mother was a descendant of Levi Strauss, the blue-jeans manufacturer. Mrs. Goldman's grandmother, Mrs. Sigmund Stern, was also a residential client and the patron of Stern Hall women's dormitory.

The Goldman house, with its gray-stained redwood exterior and concrete columns, was designed by Philadelphia-born modernist architect Joseph Esherick, who had apprenticed with Gardner Dailey. He liked humble components, and the Goldman house represented "unassertive elegance." A fairly new architect, Esherick found Frances to be intimidating, though he greatly admired how she had decorated Casa Amesti, "the wonderful house in Monterey . . . that she . . . turned into an absolutely marvelous place. But she was a pretty fierce woman. She'd run over you in nothing flat, and some kid like me—I mean, she deigned to listen to me from time to time, just barely."[11] •

OPPOSITE The spacious, high-ceilinged living room was ideal for Frances's arresting use of an overscale leaf pattern in black-and-white linen for sofas, curtains, and valances. Red throw pillows and cushions on the various chairs added seasoning.

ABOVE The glazed and skylit two-story entrance and stair hall displayed Frances's signature use of black, white, and red.

Los Angeles Turf Club

SANTA ANITA PARK

ARCADIA, CALIFORNIA · 1952

SANTA ANITA PARK IS OFTEN called America's most beautiful racecourse, and its Turf Club building—one of Frances's most celebrated public commissions—is considered the country's most elegant clubhouse. Frances would decorate its interiors in 1946 and again in 1952, the version seen here.

The Los Angeles Turf Club, headed by San Francisco dentist Dr. Charles Strub, created the Santa Anita Park complex, which opened in 1934. In 1955, *Sports Illustrated* wrote, "The Strub flair for elegance is everywhere apparent from the brown-and-black-clad bellhops to the gold-keyed wine clerk in the deep-pile carpeted Turf Club, the elite membership group of the track." (In the 1940s, Strub and his wife, Vera, would become residential clients of Frances's.) The Art Deco–style grandstand and the traditional-styled Turf Club building were designed by Gordon Kaufmann with contributions by Roland Coate. The Turf Club's architecture has been described as a mixture of American colonial, Spanish Colonial Revival, and New Orleans styles. The main salon in the club was the spacious Chandelier Room, whose decor was memorialized in a key scene in the 1954 film *A Star Is Born*. The room was named for the four massive 18th-century chandeliers, designed of crystal and Waterford glass. Frances acquired them in London in summer 1947 from the 1698 townhouse of Lord Wimbourne before it was demolished. Originally painted steel blue with white trim, the exterior has been the familiar "Santa Anita green" since at least 1946.

In their 2013 book *Racecourse Architecture*, Paul Roberts and Isabelle Taylor wrote that Santa Anita offered "a level of glamour unparalleled in America. Architecture and landscape had been harnessed to instill an image of sophistication, éclat, and propriety to the sport." Frances's two postwar renovations of the Turf Club brought the glamour quotient to its apogee during a time when Santa Anita spent $100,000 per season on floral arrangements alone and the racetrack attracted the leaders of society as well as well-heeled Hollywood celebrities like dapper regulars Fred Astaire and Cary Grant. •

TOP The Turf Club's exquisitely preserved main entrance.

ABOVE The Brazilian Room, 1955, exactly as decorated by Frances. Zuber's scenic wallpaper Les Vues de Brésil is seen on the back wall.

OPPOSITE A corner of the Chandelier Room. Swagged and fringed green curtains with enormous tassels cover the room's windows. The elaborate planters were likely designed by Frances.

ABOVE The Chandelier Room with all of its Elkins decor in a 1955 *Sports Illustrated* image showing the glittering chandeliers, long bar, parquet floor, enormous curtains, seating, and planters. In 1952, Frances refurbished the room in cool, green tones applied to the walls, window coverings, and upholstered furniture, with gray as the accent color.

OPPOSITE TOP The Directors Room was lined with antique English pine paneling Frances acquired through her friend and client Jules Stein, the Hollywood agent.

OPPOSITE BOTTOM For the ladies lounge (left), Frances selected C.W. Stockwell's wallpaper Dutchman's Pipe in silver with golden leaves to cover the ceiling and cascade down the walls. There is no record of the color scheme for this room (right), possibly another ladies lounge, but its crisply cohesive arrangement is evident.

Mr. & Mrs. Albert Schlesinger

SAN FRANCISCO, CALIFORNIA

1951

ONE OF THE MOST extraordinary collaborations between Frances and Gardner Dailey was the striking house of Mr. and Mrs. Albert Schlesinger, with its seductively eclectic rooms. The house had an atmosphere that *Vogue* magazine described as "romantically beautiful interiors."[12] The hilltop home, with its austere gray-and-white rectangular exterior, had rooms designed to look their best for nighttime entertaining. Frances was able to draw from all her experience to compose, with bravura, forward-looking rooms that integrated traditional elements, achieving something of international high style. The couple were outspoken, even contentious, clients who were very engaged in the process. Frances told photographer Fred Lyon that the Schlesingers were "curious and eager to learn. We had knock-down, drag-outs but out of that, I got some of the best solutions." Lyon, who photographed many of Frances's California commissions, recounted in interviews that he felt the "dramatic" Schlesinger living room was "one of Frances's best. The design was very pure. It was really so modern."

Albert "Speed" Schlesinger was the founder of S&C Motors, one of the nation's largest Ford auto dealerships. He was a trustee of the San Francisco Museum of Modern Art (now SFMOMA), among other civic involvements. Mrs. Schlesinger (née Irma Clayburgh) was a strong influence on her daughter, the international style icon Nan Kempner. *San Francisco Examiner* society columnist Susan Smith noted in a November 1951 column that Mrs. Schlesinger had a "strong predilection for red, pink, white, and black," and asked that these colors be used. According to Smith, Frances was happy to comply as "these happened to be her favorite colors" as well. •

RIGHT The spacious living room had walls painted the faintest pink (which read as white in color photos). A gros point 1673 English rug in red, gold, turquoise, and black provided the color key to the entire room.

LEFT A view from the second-floor reception hall into the living room. The rich reds, pinks, blacks, and golds of the furniture and brightly colored carnations are glimpsed through the gilded doors. One of a pair of 17th-century stools with turned legs is covered in a burgundy silk damask fabric. A boldly patterned tribal rug is a powerful statement on the ebonized-wood floor.

OPPOSITE "The dining room is black and gold, a severe but stunning combination," remarked Susan Smith in her 1951 *San Francisco Examiner* column. The setting was an off-white room with a contrasting black teak floor with diagonal brass inlay. The palm-form floor lamp was inspired by Serge Roche. Frances designed the armless chairs, interpreting a Frank model; she likely created the black-lacquered dining table and banquettes as well. The chairs and the banquettes, with their up-to-the-minute forms, were upholstered in a sparkling hand-woven Dorothy Liebes textile with black, white, and gold threads.

OPPOSITE Side view of the second-floor reception hall looking toward a service hall that contained the powder room. The glimmer of a 19th-century gilded Burmese Buddha centers a composition that included Frances's white shell sconces.

ABOVE The master bedroom was decorated in celadon green, with shimmering Dorothy Liebes material covering the sofa and throw pillows. For contrast, red-woven Liebes fabric covers the two Louis XVI chairs.

LEFT Mrs. Schlesinger is shown in the living room, which had what columnist Susan Smith called "marvelous antiques." Behind her, an Adam settee covered in red satin anchored the seating area.

SurfRider Hotel

HONOLULU, HAWAII · 1952

TO SATISFY THE TASTES of travelers who preferred a less formal and more modern atmosphere than the Royal Hawaiian Hotel, the Matson company commissioned Gardner Dailey and Frances to create the SurfRider, the first modern high-rise hotel on Waikiki. Dailey provided interior spaces with his customary clean-lined proportions and high ceilings. Frances would lean into the midcentury modern aesthetic that was becoming more prevalent but would instill the SurfRider with an atmosphere of both simple glamour and Polynesian whimsy.

As she had done with the World War II–era hostess uniforms at a junior officer's club, Frances almost certainly designed SurfRider staff uniforms to coordinate with the decor, as seen, for example, in the outfit worn by an elevator operator in the photo opposite. The public spaces could be likened to theater sets with the staff as the performers.

The best way to conjure the SurfRider's atmosphere is through the eyes of someone who saw the Elkins decor firsthand. When interviewed in 2022, Santa Barbara interior designer Penelope Bianchi shared her vivid memories of sailing from California on the *Matsonia* to stay at the SurfRider: "I was 13 years old in 1960. My mother had been a big fan of Frances Elkins. She had friends in Pebble Beach whose homes had been decorated by Frances." Her mother, who had lived in Hawaii in the 1930s, wanted to see the SurfRider. "I remember my mother saying Frances had not done anything like that before: 'This is her expedition into modern.' The colors and the way she tied things together, like the red lampshades. What a talented woman. All those elements, like how the flowers matched the lampshades. It was a stunning, stunning hotel. It was elegant modern. That building had a lot of classical elements that were sort of combined into a modern style. It was a really beautiful hotel. Very unusual."

Bianchi also went on to describe some of the hotel's other unique features: "I remember the mirrors, the unusual light fixtures, the Tiki gods. She was very ahead of her time." •

OPPOSITE Against deeply colored teal green walls, bright orange-red details provide energetic accents to unify the design. Comfortable seating in a harmonizing soft gray-green lent a feeling of serenity and refuge. The columns were painted in creamy yellows with motifs representing leaves or boomerangs. On the terrazzo floors were large rugs of woven matting.

ABOVE The cocktail lounge's dark stained-wood paneling and ceiling panels are reminiscent of the interior of a traditional Japanese house. More of the hotel's Polynesian designs were incorporated on painted wall panels, on wall sconces, and on the painted border above the bar. A South Seas or Asian mood is apparent in the hanging basket light fixtures and woven blinds.

OPPOSITE TOP The soft blue-green was the "comfort food" of this particular space. One of sculptor Cecilia Graham's Tiki statues is seen at right, its face oriented toward the ocean-front corridor. The red-and-white wall sconces, another nod to Polynesian culture, have "eyes" painted on them. Frances and Gardner Dailey may have collaborated to create the upholstered furnishings in

the lobby and the seating, beds, and tables in the guest rooms. Frances likely designed the lobby's tables and the cane-back chairs at the writing tables.

OPPOSITE BOTTOM LEFT The seating area in a larger guest suite, with reddish-orange shades (similar to the red used in the lobby) on unusual spiral black-metal table lamps.

OPPOSITE BOTTOM RIGHT Teal and orange were chosen for the upholstered seating, including the curved-back designs inspired by captain's chairs. The bartenders were color-coordinated in orange and black, while the vertical wooden ribs on the front of the bar are detailed with teal and orange spots.

ENDNOTES

1 In 1952, BOAC introduced the de Havilland DH.106 Comet, the world's first commercial jet airplane. Boeing Aircraft Company's first commercial jet airplane, the 707, was introduced in 1955.

2 Joan Chatfield-Taylor, "Sister Parish on Taste: You Can't Acquire It," *San Francisco Chronicle*, October 21, 1981.

3 In late May 1930, David and Katherine were touring Europe and planning to attend the Stockholm Exhibition of 1930, a groundbreaking fair which exhibited modernist Scandinavian architecture in a cheerful, holiday setting. Katherine was killed in an automobile accident when the couple were maneuvering their brand-new Packard on a rain-slicked road in France, and crashed into a tree. Katherine had a premonition of danger during the fateful drive and insisted on stopping at a wayside chapel to light a candle an hour before she died. Eerily, a full-page photo of the lovely Katherine, apparently dressed in black, and used to publicize her new novel *The Crystal Icicle*, would appear in the June 7 *Vogue*, an issue which was probably being printed at the time she died. Adler was bereft and barely able to work over the next year.

4 In late summer 1939, Frances, her daughter Katie, her mother Therese Adler, brother David and cousin Mrs. Alfred M. Mendel were vacationing in France when they were caught up in one of the first moments of the second world war. On September 3, France declared war on Germany. Frances, very aware of the anti-Semitism of the Nazis, rushed to secure passage to America for herself, Katie, and Mrs. Mendel. She had to leave behind her ailing mother, who was being treated at the American hospital in Paris. With David's help, Therese was moved to Etretat on the French coast, where she died on September 17. Frances, meanwhile, had escaped under perilous conditions. It was reported in one of the San Francisco newspapers on September 24 that among other prominent San Francisco society figures fleeing Europe, Frances was on the high seas, bound for home. But as she later told a magazine writer, she had "narrowly escaped being trapped by Hitler's hordes when they over-ran France. She returned to America under conditions that made the old time steerage passage resemble a trip on a luxury liner." ("Pentraits: Por Qué Mrs. Elkins?" by Jack Morris, *What's Doing*, July 1946.)

5 "The Intellectual Climate of San Francisco," *Harper's Bazaar*, February 1947.

6 That year, she was decorating the expansive country homes of Mrs. Clark, Mrs. Reed, and the Joseph Cudahys; the four-story townhouse of the Wolcott Blairs; the elegant apartments of the Potter Palmers and Mrs. Ely; and Joseph Ryerson's new penthouse library, her first use of Jean-Michel Frank furniture. She was continuing to decorate the California homes of Hester Hately (later Griffin) and George Cameron, and the North Shore homes of the Laurance Armours, the Robert Mandels and the Albert Laskers, as well as the house of her aunt Nettie and uncle Charles Stonehill. In the contract sector, Frances was furnishing the exclusive Cypress Point Golf Club, the picturesque Del Monte Lodge, and the understated and gentlemanly Lee Higginson banking offices in Chicago's new Art Deco Board of Trade building. She was also assisting David Adler in fitting out the ultramodern Attic Club in another Chicago Art Deco tower, the Field Building The Hotel Del Monte, an ongoing client, would ask Frances to fashion a new sun parlor. In an April 2, 1930 letter to her "Aunt Net," Frances wrote that "Quite a lot of work is in prospect if I don't carry the grand piano around and put myself out of commission. I am going to do the Foreman Apartment that Dave is doing and Mrs. Florsheim's and perhaps the Lester Armour house which is very large. Out here I am going to do the lodge . . . and have been asked to do a Ritz in San Francisco. I am not very crazy about doing a hotel since the medium is very limited. Things get shabby pretty quickly."

7 *Monterey Peninsula Herald*, April 6, 1939.

8 An architectural practice in the San Francisco Bay Area, 1938–1996, by Joseph Esherick, Regional Oral History Office; William Turnbull and Suzanne Riess, Bancroft Library.

9 An April 1955 *Sports Illustrated* feature on the recently redecorated Turf Club was headlined "Trackside Luxury." [complete cite]

10 Morris, ibid [or id]/

11 An architectural practice in the San Francisco Bay Area, 1938–1996, by Joseph Esherick, Regional Oral History Office; William Turnbull and Suzanne Riess, Bancroft Library.

12 "San Francisco House," *Vogue*, April 15, 1952.

CLIENT LIST

NEW YORK, NEW YORK
Mr. and Mrs. Julien Chaqueneau, c. 1933–35*
Mrs. Evelyn Marshall Field, 1935–36
Mr. and Mrs. Albert Lasker, 1946*
Mr. and Mrs. Levin, c. 1930s–1940s
Mr. and Mrs. Harold Ruckman Mixsell, c. 1936–40*
Mr. and Mrs. William Paley, 1935*
Mr. and Mrs. Abram Poole, c. 1930
Mr. and Mrs. Barclay Warburton II, c. 1935

CENTERVILLE, NEW YORK
Mr. and Mrs. William K. Vanderbilt II, 1936

FISHERS ISLAND, NEW YORK
Mr. and Mrs. Van Horn Ely, Jr., 1931

MT. KISCO, NEW YORK
Mr. and Mrs. DeWitt Wallace, c. 1948–1953

MANHASSET, NEW YORK
Mr. and Mrs. William Paley, 1939*

SYOSSET, NEW YORK
Mrs. Evelyn Marshall Field, 1931–1935

IPSWICH, MASSACHUSETTS
Mr. and Mrs. Richard Teller Crane, Jr., c. 1927–1931

HAVERFORD, PENNSYLVANIA
Mr. and Mrs. Van Horn Ely, Sr., 1931
Mrs. Van Horn Ely, Sr., 1937

PAOLI, PENNSYLVANIA
Mr. and Mrs. Van Horn Ely, Jr., 1949–1953

RADNOR/VILLANOVA, PENNSYLVANIA
Mr. and Mrs. Van Horn Ely, Jr., c. 1931–1948

MIAMI, FLORIDA
Mr. and Mrs. John Hertz, 1930s
Mr. and Mrs. Albert Lasker, 1930s

CHICAGO
Mr. and Mrs. Benjamin Becker, c. 1932
Mr. and Mrs. Wolcott Blair, 1930
Mr. and Mrs. Richard Teller Crane, Jr., 1930
Mr. and Mrs. Edward Cudahy, c. 1927–30
Mr. and Mrs. Joseph Cudahy, c. 1930
Mrs. Carolyn Morse Ely, 1930–36
Mr. and Mrs. Harold Foreman, c. 1928
Mr. and Mrs. Charles Goodspeed, 1927
Mrs. Frederick Mandel, c. 1931*
Mr. and Mrs. Max Markwell, c. 1920s–30s
Mr. and Mrs. Potter Palmer II, 1929–30
Mr. and Mrs. Joseph Ryerson, c. 1921–1930
Mr. and Mrs. Denis Sullivan, 1935*

CARY, ILLINOIS
Mr. and Mrs. John Hertz, 1930s

GLENCOE, ILLINOIS
Mr. and Mrs. Leigh Block, 1940 (with Samuel Marx)*
Mr. and Mrs. Edwin Foreman, c. 1930
Mr. and Mrs. Gerhard Foreman, 1930s
Mr. and Mrs. Charles Stonehill, c. 1921–1929
Mr. and Mrs. Jesse Strauss, 1921

HIGHLAND PARK, ILLINOIS
Mr. and Mrs. Leonard Florsheim, 1930
Mr. and Mrs. Robert Mandel, 1928
Mrs. Max Markwell, 1930s
Mr. and Mrs. Roy Wyle, c. 1939
Mr. and Mrs. Roy Wyle, c. 1949 (with Marjorie Thorsch)*

LAKE BLUFF, ILLINOIS
Mr. and Mrs. Lester Armour, 1931–36
Mr. and Mrs. William McCormick Blair, 1926
Mrs. Carolyn Morse Ely, 1925
Mr. and Mrs. DeForest Hulburd, 1928

LAKE FOREST, ILLINOIS
Mr. and Mrs. Laurance Armour, 1928–1936

Mrs. Leola Armour, c. 1949
Mrs. J. Ogden Armour, 1934–36
Mr. and Mrs. Richard Bentley, c. 1930
Mr. and Mrs. Walter Brewster, c. 1930s
Mr. and Mrs. Joseph Cudahy, 1921*
Mr. and Mrs. Joseph Cudahy, 1930
Mr. and Mrs. Joseph Cudahy, c. 1935*
Mr. and Mrs. Dexter Cummings, c. 1929–37
Mrs. Albert B. Dick, c. 1939
Mr. and Mrs. Edison Dick, 1932–35
Ms. Gwethalyn Jones, c. 1930s
Mr. and Mrs. Stanley Keith, c. 1930
Mr. and Mrs. Albert Lasker, 1926–36
Mr. and Mrs. Cyrus McCormick, c. 1930s
Mr. and Mrs. Joseph Medill Patterson, 1930s
Mrs. Kersey Coates Reed, 1929–1932
Mr. and Mrs. Henry N. Rowley, c. 1930
Mrs. Leverett Thompson, 1930s
Mr. and Mrs. Samuel Walker, 1935

LIBERTYVILLE, ILLINOIS
Mr. and Mrs. David Adler, 1920s
Mr. David Adler, 1941
Mrs. Isaac D. Adler, 1930s

MILLBURN, ILLINOIS
Mr. and Mrs. Albert B. Dick, Jr., c. 1934*

WINNETKA, ILLINOIS
Mr. and Mrs. Louis Kuppenheimer, Jr., 1937

MIAMI, OKLAHOMA
Mr. and Mrs. George Coleman, Jr., 1936

SAN FRANCISCO, CALIFORNIA
Mrs. Russell Ach, c. 1930s
Mr. Raymond Armsby, 1940
Mrs. Claire Brown, 1940–41
Mr. and Mrs. William W. Crocker, 1948
Mr. and Mrs. Gardner Dailey, 1936–1945
Mr. Gardner Dailey, 1949
Mr. and Mrs. Albert Ehrman, c. 1930
Mr. and Mrs. Sidney Ehrman, c. 1930s–1940s
Mr. and Mrs. Herbert Fleishhacker, 1940s
Mr. and Mrs. Peter Folger, 1945
Mr. and Mrs. Richard Goldman, 1952
Mr. and Mrs. Morgan Gunst, 1948–53
Mr. and Mrs. Walter Haas, 1949
Mr. and Mrs. Frederick Hellman, 1938
Mr. and Mrs. Felix Kahn, c. 1939
Mrs. and Mrs. Bruce Kelham, 1940s
Mr. and Mrs. Lewis Lapham, 1942–47
Mr. and Mrs. Roger Lapham, Jr., c. 1947*
Mrs. Clarence Lindner, c. 1947–1952
Mr. and Mrs. Charles Oelrich Martin, c. 1950
Mrs. Kate Felton Neilson, c. 1929
Mr. and Mrs. Carl Raiss, 1930s
Mr. and Mrs. Henry Potter Russell, c. 1948
Mr. and Mrs. Albert Schlesinger, 1951
Mr. and Mrs. James Schwabacher, 1936
Mr. and Mrs. Robert Sinton, 1951
Mr. and Mrs. Stanley Sinton, c. 1950
Mrs. Sigmund Stern, 1952
Mr. Whitney Warren, Jr., 1936–52
Mr. and Mrs. Robert Wiel, 1950
Mr. and Mrs. James D. Zellerbach, 1937, 1945

ATHERTON, CALIFORNIA
Mr. Alan Fleishhacker, 1941
Mr. and Mrs. Carl Raiss, 1930s
Mr. and Mrs. Edward Topham, 1948

BELVEDERE, CALIFORNIA
Mr. and Mrs. McKinley Bissinger, 1952*
Mr. and Mrs. Stewart Hopps, 1952

HILLSBOROUGH, CALIFORNIA
Mr. and Mrs. Charles Blyth, 1936*
Mr. and Mrs. Hillyer Brown, 1937
Mr. and Mrs. George Cameron, 1929–1937, 1949
Mrs. Celia Tobin Clark, 1929–1936
Mr. and Mrs. Sheldon Cooper, c. 1937*
Mr. and Mrs. William W. Crocker, 1930s
Mr. and Mrs. Thomas Finigan, c. 1930
Mr. and Mrs. Bernard Ford, 1953
Dr. and Mrs. Irvin Gardner, 1949
Mr. and Mrs. Wellington Henderson, 1948
Mr. and Mrs. Samuel Kahn, 1936–37
Mr. and Mrs. Decker McAllister, c. 1936
Mr. and Mrs. Donald McLeod Lewis, c. 1950
Mr. and Mrs. Paul Albert Miller, c. 1950*

Mr. and Mrs. Robert Roos, Sr., 1930s
Mr. and Mrs. Robert Roos, Jr., 1940s
Mr. and Mrs. George Pope, Jr., 1936*
Mr. and Mrs. Porter Sesnon, 1930s
Mr. and Mrs. Henry Sicular, 1949*
Mr. and Mrs. Laurence Strassburger, c. 1930s
Mr. and Mrs. Charles Thieriot, 1940s
Mr. and Mrs. Roland Tognazzini, 1940s

LARKSPUR, CALIFORNIA
Mr. and Mrs. Eugene Elkus, c. 1937

LOS ALTOS HILLS, CALIFORNIA
Mr. and Mrs. Milton Haas, c. 1938

LOS GATOS, CALIFORNIA
Mr. and Mrs. Michel Weill, 1940*

MENLO PARK, CALIFORNIA
Mr. and Mrs. Richard Zellerbach, 1951

MILLBRAE, CALIFORNIA
Mr. and Mrs. Ogden Mills, 1930s

PIEDMONT, CALIFORNIA
Mr. and Mrs. Edward Crossan, 1952

WOODSIDE, CALIFORNIA
Mr. and Mrs. Charles de Bretteville, 1950
Mr. and Mrs. Peter Folger, 1945
Mrs. and Mrs. Bruce Kelham, 1940s
Mr. and Mrs. Atholl McBean, 1936*

CARMEL, CALIFORNIA
Mr. and Mrs. Harrison Godwin, c. 1946
Mr. and Mrs. Harold Mack, 1940s

CARMEL VALLEY, CALIFORNIA
Mrs. Edmonds Dexter, 1941*
Mr. and Mrs. Samuel F.B. Morse, c. 1929–1938
Mr. and Mrs. Henry Potter Russell, 1930s–1940s

MONTEREY, CALIFORNIA
Mr. and Mrs. James B. Black, 1940
Mr. and Mrs. Harold Mack, c. 1928
Mr. and Mrs. Gouverneur Morris, c. 1925–29
Mr. and Mrs. Carl Stanley, 1920s–1930s
Mr. and Mrs. Harry W. Toulmin, c. 1922
Susan Viola Wood, c. 1925–27
Mr. and Mrs. Frank Work, 1949

PEBBLE BEACH, CALIFORNIA
Mrs. E.H. Baldwin
Mr. and Mrs. Thomas Bunn, 1940
Mr. and Mrs. William H. Burnham, Jr., 1937
Mr. and Mrs. Louis Cates, 1941
Mr. and Mrs. John Chapman, 1938
Mr. and Mrs. George Coleman, Jr., 1946
Mr. and Mrs. John Cravens, 1921*
Mr. and Mrs. Tirey Ford, c. 1946
Mr. and Mrs. Arthur Hately/Col. and Mrs. Allen Griffin,
    1926–1949
Mr. and Mrs. Arthur Hately, Jr., 1946
Mr. and Mrs. Charles Howard
Mr. and Mrs. William Hudson, c. 1940
Mr. and Mrs. Harry Hunt, 1930–1934
Mr. and Mrs. Robert Hunter, 1930s
Mr. and Mrs. John Magee, 1930
Mr. and Mrs. Samuel F.B. Morse, c. 1930–1936
Mr. and Mrs. Daniel Murphy, 1930s
Ms. Bernardine Murphy, 1940s–1950s
Col. and Mrs. John Hudson Poole, 1921*
Mr. and Mrs. Robert Stanton, 1940
Mr. and Mrs. Hampton Stewart, Jr.
Mr. and Mrs. Eric Tyrrell–Martin, 1930s
Mr. and Mrs. Paul Winslow, 1948
Mr. and Mrs. E.B. Young

SANTA CRUZ, CALIFORNIA
Mr. and Mrs. W.E. Gallway, Pasatiempo Country Club,
    1932
Ms. Marion Hollins, Pasatiempo Country Club, 1931
Mr. and Mrs. Earle Kaplansky, Pasatiempo Country Club,
    1931
Mr. and Mrs. Samuel Randall, 1948
Mr. and Mrs. William Van Antwerp, c. 1930*

MODESTO, CALIFORNIA
Mr. and Mrs. Ernest Gallo, 1941
Mr. and Mrs. Richard S. Hiatt, 1939

RUTHERFORD, CALIFORNIA
Mr. and Mrs. Georges de Latour, c. 1929–1940

SANTA BARBARA, CALIFORNIA
Mrs. Henry E. Bothin 1930s
Mr. and Mrs. Charles Jackson, Jr., 1932 (with Cornelia
    Conger)*
Mr. and Mrs. Malcolm McNaughton, c. 1950*
Mr. and Mrs. Robert Stewart Odell, c. 1940s
Mr. and Mrs. Joseph Ryerson, Jr., 1936–1953
Mrs. Harry W. Toulmin, 1952*

BEL AIR, CALIFORNIA
Mr. and Mrs. Louis B. Mayer, 1949*
Mr. and Mrs. Sol Wurtzel, 1931–1939

BEVERLY GLEN, CALIFORNIA
Mr. and Mrs. Jules Stein, c. 1939*

BEVERLY HILLS, CALIFORNIA
Mr. Algernon Barbee, 1936
Mr. and Mrs. Robert Mandel, 1936
Mr. and Mrs. Edward G. Robinson, 1941–1944
Mr. and Mrs. David O. Selznick, 1937–1941

GLENDALE, CALIFORNIA
Mr. John Gilbert and Ms. Ina Claire, 1929–30

HOLMBY HILLS, CALIFORNIA
Ms. Irene Dunne (Mrs. Francis Griffin), c. 1939–1949
Mr. and Mrs. Harry Kunin, 1949

LOS ANGELES, CALIFORNIA
Mr. and Mrs. Herbert Hiestand, 1936 (assisting Edna
    Hiestand)
Ms. Bernardine Murphy, 1940s–1950s
Mr. and Mrs. Daniel Murphy, 1930s
Ms. Sue Sinnott, 1940s–1950s
Ms. Norma Shearer (exact location and date unknown)

PACIFIC PALISADES, CALIFORNIA
Mr. and Mrs. Ben Goetz, 1941
Mr. and Mrs. Richard Jewett Schweppe, 1930s

PASADENA, CALIFORNIA
Mr. and Mrs. Allen Dragge, c. 1947
Mr. and Mrs. Leonard Firestone. c. 1940s
Col. and Mrs. John Hudson Poole, c. 1934

SAN MARINO, CALIFORNIA
Dr. and Mrs. Charles H. Strub, c. 1944

NASSAU, BAHAMAS
Mr. and Mrs. Hollis Baker, 1948

SUSSEX, ENGLAND
Mr. and Mrs. Gilbert Miller, 1939*

VENICE, ITALY
Mr. Carlos de Beistegui (assisting Mr. Beistegui), 1948*

TAXCO, MEXICO
Mr. David Adler, c. 1936–1944

PUBLIC COMMISSIONS/
CONTRACT WORK
Ambassador Hotel, Los Angeles, CA, c. 1930
Ambassador East Hotel, Chicago, IL, 1951 (assisting
    Dorothy Liebes)*
American Women's Voluntary Services, Naval Officers'
    Mess, Hillsborough, CA, 1944
American Women's Voluntary Services, Junior Officers'
    Club, San Francisco, CA 1942
Airway Ranch model home, Carmel Valley, CA, 1942
The Attic Club, Chicago, IL, 1933
Baker Furniture Company, Grand Rapids, MI,
    c. 1945–1950
Barbizon Hotel for Women, New York, NY, 1934
Barbizon-Plaza Hotel, New York, NY 1934
Beach Club, Pebble Beach, CA, 1930 and 1949
Beverly Hills Hotel, Beverly Hills, CA, c. 1945–1951
Burlingame Country Club, Hillsborough, CA,
    c. 1948
Cabin Crafts, Inc., New York, NY and Dalton, GA,
    c. 1944–1953
California Golf Club, South San Francisco, CA,
    c. 1948
Cardinal Hotel, Palo Alto, CA, c. 1948
Carmel USO, Carmel, CA, 1942
Carmel Valley Inn, Carmel Valley, CA, 1947 (with
    Eleanor Forbes and David Prince)
Claremont Country Club, Oakland, CA, 1947
Clift Hotel, San Francisco, CA, c. 1949–1952
Ann Coleman debutante party, Burlingame Country
    Club, 1952
Colonial Drapery Fabrics., Inc., New York, NY, c. 1945
Colton Hall, Monterey, CA, 1940s

INDEX

ACKNOWLEDGMENTS

DEDICATED TO MY PARENTS

WILLIAM THURSTON POWELL AND RUTH ESTHER POWELL

I AM PARTICULARLY INDEBTED TO David Sprott Boyd and William Elkins Boyd, Frances Elkins's grandsons, for their enthusiastic support, background information on Frances including family lore, and broad access to their personal archives. This book would be much less rich without their heirloom photos of Elkins interiors and of Frances herself, as well as rare memorabilia. I also thank David's partner, Meg Starr, and Bill's wife, Kjorina Boyd. And I acknowledge two other members of Frances's extended family, Carol Zsolnay and Susan Schreiber Mandel, for sharing rare information about the Adler and Hyman families, respectively.

I am grateful to have had the full cooperation of the Frances Adler Elkins archives at Monterey Peninsula College and the following individuals: Diane Bower, Mary Nelson, Denise Sallee, Wendy Good, Elizabeth Thomas, Amelia Converse, and Sunshine Giesler. The materials in the archives were donated by David Boyd and Milton Johnson.

I feel very lucky that my editor at Rizzoli is Ellen Nidy, who has had a strong belief in me and in this project. She became the anchor who brought clarity and focus in marshalling what had been largely theoretical into a fully actualized book. I also thank managing editor Lynn Scrabis for her enthusiastic input; publisher Charles Miers, for his enthusiasm and ongoing support during the extensive book preparation; and designer Sarah Gifford, for her masterful layouts and typography throughout the monograph.

I wish to give special thanks to the following people:

Stephen Salny, for providing constant encouragement, for sharing his vast knowledge of Frances Elkins and David Adler, and for generously lending photos and archival materials. It was Steve who told me in 2008 I should do a book on Frances, which then seemed an overwhelming task. He helped connect me to many people who could further my understanding of Frances's career;

Dupuy Warrick Reed, whose assistance with writing and framing the story was so invaluable. His comprehension of the history of interior design and art history was of great help to me, as was his willingness to share his many 1983 interviews with Frances Elkins's clients, colleagues, and family;

Diane Dorrans Saeks, design author and style journalist, for her early faith and constant support for my book, her enthusiasm for Frances Elkins, and her introduction to Rizzoli;

Steven Sutor, whose professional background as an interior designer helped me to appreciate various aspects of Frances's interiors. My many dialogues with Steven were an important sounding board for my writing;

Diane Bower, emeritus Interior Design faculty 1974-2002, Monterey Peninsula College. Diane kindly shared the results of her ASID-grant-funded research into Frances Elkins, her large selection of Elkins research materials, and her deep knowledge of Frances's home Casa Amesti;

Professor Julianne Burton-Carvajal, who arranged for me to give four lectures on Frances Elkins and to be part of an Elkins roundtable discussion during an Elkins tribute weekend she organized in Monterey.

I appreciate Julianne's seasoned input in helping me craft the decades chapters and her deep awareness of Monterey history and architecture;

Pauline Metcalf, design historian, for sharing her scholarly understanding of women interior designers, including Frances Elkins and Syrie Maugham, and her extensive grasp of architectural periods and the history of American decorating in the first half of the 20th century;

Jerry Welling, for imparting his knowledge of Frances Elkins gleaned from Nelle Currie and other members of Frances's circle. I also thank Guy Rodriguez, Jerry's partner, for his kindness and encouragement;

James Shearron, for his architect's insight into the collaborations of Frances Elkins and David Adler and his familiarity with the Chicago-area families who hired the Adler siblings;

Kerry Busby, an interior designer who has done a great deal of research for me on Frances Elkins's clients;

Hutton Wilkinson, jewelry and interior designer, for making available to me many rare and important archival images of Frances's interiors taken by Duquette.

I am thankful for the following professionals who have shared their wisdom which enabled me to describe Frances's interiors: Ed Hardy, Peter Gambito and Al Ruschmeyer, Peter McCourt, Jerry Janssen, Charlotte von Hardenburgh and Alexa Griffith-Winton, J. Carolle Thibault-Pomerantz, Susan Hill Dolan and Jared Goss.

I want to thank photo restorer Dave Petranovic for his superb adjustments of hundreds of images; Tony Molatore and Gawain Weaver, for making high-quality scans of well over 2,000 photos, including stereo views, using precision technology; master colorist Victor Mascaro, for his new colorizations of Yerba Buena Club images and his restorations of two Schlesinger house photos; and artist Joe Dea, for creating new paintings of Frances's childhood home and of her early work decorating the Jesse Strauss dining room. Color consultant John Kitchener was a vital resource in identifying many of the precise colors Frances used.

I am tremendously indebted to the Samuel F.B. Morse and Thomas Bunn families for allowing still-intact Frances Elkins interiors to be photographed for this book: Ellen Osborne, Charley Osborne, Polly Osborne and Susan Osborne; and Jody Bunn and Chris Bunn. I appreciate photographer Russell MacMasters for taking exquisite images of the Morse summer home and the Bunn Pebble Beach residence. I also thank Jim Jackson and realtor Suzanne Perkins for kindly allowing me to take two tours of the Charles Jackson, Jr. house when it was for sale with all of its 1932 furnishings and decor completely preserved. I am fortunate to have been able to conduct several interviews with photographer Fred Lyon, who shared many memories of Frances Elkins, and who helped prepare for this book more than twenty of his images of Elkins interiors.

The following Elkins clients, and descendants and relatives of clients, made immeasurable contributions to the book: Joan Hately Anthony, Jean Reddy Armour, Caroline E. Bassett, Stephen Bent, Charles Black, Jr., Chris Bunn, Jody Bunn, Nathalie Bunn, Leslie de Bretteville, Linda de Espirlet, Barbara Hately DuPont,,Van Horn Ely III, Peter M. Folger, Joseph E. Gallo, Marie Gallo, Barbara Gardner, Alexander Gunst, Sterling Morton Hamill, Jonathan Hately, Peggy Henschel, Tom Henschel, Barbara Herst, John Hermann, Ariel Hermann, Jesse Hiestand,, Harlow and Susan Higinbotham, Harry and Monika Hunt, Virginia Strub Kelly, Patricia Tobin Kubal, Bud Kuppenheimer, Lewis Lapham, Jr., Sharon Leib, Kitty Margolis, Susan Schreiber-Mandel and Jeff Mandel, John and Susie Mitchell, Liz Morten, Sterling Morton, Charley Osborne, Ellen Osborne, Polly Osborne, Susan Osborne, Heather Phillips, John Raiss, Ginevra Ralph, Peter Reed, Page and Emily Roos, Ethan Russell, Daniel Selznick, Mary Morse Shaw, Alexandra Shiva, Barbara Sinton Wilson, Doug and Wendy Sinton, Fred Stanley, Ann-Marie Streibich, Dagmar Sullivan, Walter Sullivan, Ned Topham, Lowry White, Susan Zellerbach, and Susan Zurcher.

I also wish to thank these descendants of Frances Elkins's staff: Jim Costello, grandson of Frances's office manager Harriet Weill, and Jim's mother, Nancy Costello; Jayne Gasperson and her son, Gary Gasperson, the daughter and grandson of Frances's "man Friday" Lee Dix; and Carolyn Gold and Judith Schmidt, the granddaughters of Frances's cabinetmaker Myron Oliver.

My sincerest gratitude to the following friends and family who have been there for me in numerous ways (in alphabetical order): Suzanna Allen, Nancy Arvold, Catherine Birk, Michael Collins, Robert Emig, Peter Gambito, John Kitchener, Linda Kutner, Gina Loren, Jack McCarty, Jeanine Olson, Robert Palmer, Cynthia Peña, my sister Lisa Powell, Steve Shorb, Andrew Sokolsky, Helaine Tregenza, and Hella Tsaconas.

Last but not least, I need to acknowledge the following individuals representing many archives, companies, libraries and organizations. Without their contributions the book would be a shadow of itself visually and informationally: Kevin Abing, James Archer Abbott, Michael Henry Adams, Paul Adamson, Kelly Allen, Carley C. Altenburger, Morex Arai, Stephanie Arias, Steve Atchison, Susan Augustine, Quentin Bacon, Lois Baisley, Bob Baker, James Ballowe, Chris Barker, Darin Barnes, Elizabeth Barratt, Richard Ferson Barrett, Albert Bartridge, Jim Bartsch, Alison Bassett, Robert Beck, Barbara Becker, Paula Beckman, Susan Benjamin, Paul Bergmann, Irene Berry, Penelope Bianchi, Greg Bianchini, Biarritz Mediatheque, Matt Bischoff, Doug Black, Dr. Robert and Jean Black, Anne Blecksmith, Steven Boggs, Jennifer Boles, Dick Bories, Hal Boucher, Lisa Singleton Boudiette, Marisa Bourgoin, Charles Boyd, Deborah Brackstone, Lisa Bradford, Brittany Bradley, Barbara Briggs-Anderson, Sean Briscoe, Thomas Britt, Julie Britt, Lynn Brittner, Robert Brooks, Judy Bross, DeSoto Brown, Marianne Brown, Steven Brown, Charles Burger, Shirley Burgett, Scott Burgh, Julie Cain, Samantha Cairo-Toby, David J. Califf, Ashley Callahan, Stephen Calloway, Fran Cappelletti, Thomas Carey, Jim Carroll, Pamela Casey, Emiliano Castellano, Cynthia Cathcart, Gisèle Chalaye, Erin Chase, Chicago.Designslinger, Chicago History Museum, Tom Clendening, Meg Clovis, Russ Cohen, Leslie Cook, Armon Cooper, Dennis Copeland, Jen Correia, Shanti Corrigan, Kim Coventry, Mary Crowe, Crown Gardens & Archives/ Whitfield-Murray Historical Society, Jewel Cummins, Curt Teich Postcard Archives Collection / Newberry Library, Jill D'Allessandro, Elizabeth Dalton, Alexandra Daniloff, Abby Dansiger, Juliet Stein Davies, Gary Davis, Trish Davis, Mike Dawson, Tom Deaton, Dr. Eric and Teresa Del Piero, Amber DelaCruz, Patrick Dragonette, Tom Deaton, JT de la Torre, Deborah Dell'Isola, Anita Denz, Missy Derse, Julie DeVere, Jennifer Detweiller, Alexandra Dimitroff, Ted and Stacey Dobos, Katie Quinn Donovan, Rachael Dreyer, William Drucker, Keira Dubowsky, Hank Dunlop, Lisa Dunseth, The Duquette Foundation Archives, Oksana Dykyj, John Eastberg, John Eckert, Jeffrey Eger, Hannah Elder, Simon Elliott, Emily Evans Eerdmans, Katherine Ets-Hokin, Martin Filler, Richard Finch, Tom Fritz Studio, Dr. Douglas Flamming, Manuel Flores, Alexia Fontaine, Mary Forney, Scott Fuller, Melinda Gandara, Cathy Garrett, Markie Gayles, Tom GillmorThomas Gleason, Helaine Glick, Jane Glover, Leslie Goddard, Geoffrey Goldberg, Susan Goldstein, Don Goodhue, Freeman Gosden, Jr., Jennifer Gotti, Julie Grahame, Krista L. Gray, Michael Green, Teri Green, John A. Greenwald, Andrea Grimes, Sue Grinols, Jeff Groff, Cliff Grost, Jean M. Grost, Rose Guerrero, Allen Gutterman, Neil Harris, Rebeca Hatcher, Luisa Haddad,

Alexa Hampton, Duane Hampton, Michael Hampton, Neil Harris, Brent Hartman, Rita M. Hassert, Amy Hathaway, Pat Hathaway, Steve Hauk, Stephen Headley, Nancy Heimer, Jenny Heffernon, Erik Helweg-Larsen, Gabe Herzog, Alan Hess, Tom High, Cole Hill, Scott Himmel, Caroline L. Hirsch (Esto), Helga Horner, Neal Hotelling Jeff Hull, Christine Hult-Lewis, Barry Hutner, Jay Hyland, Fred Iberri, Salwa Ismail, Eric Ismay, Wendy S. Israel, Heidi Jamison, Richard Janick (MAARA), Drew Johnson, Alicia Jordanova, Daniel Jordanov, Aliya Kalla, Barbara Karpf, Victoria Kastner, Kathleen Kay, John Keller, Peg Kemper, Nathan Kerr, David Kessler, Linda Kiel, Ina Kielley, Lorraine Kilkenny, Edna Kimbro, Don Kinsella, Anne Kirk, Lorna K. Kirwan, Harry Kolb, Judith Knipple, Fred Koch, Harry Kolb, Jim Kovacs, Dee Dee Kramer), Lynn Blocker Krantz, Marci Krause, Susan Kriete, Kristine Krueger, Shellie Labell, Jonathan LaCrosse, Michael Maire Lange, Harmony Larke, Julia Larson, Ashley Latona, Bruce Laverty, Colleen Layton, Kevin B. Leonard, Karen E Lesney-Lysanyuk, Katie Levi, Russ Levikow, Glen Leroux, Adam Lewis, Wendy Lewis, Libertyville Historical Society, Maggie Lidz, Brady Lindsey, Kathy Lo, Waverly Lowell, Laura Luce, Valera Lyles, Dee MacDonald, Laura MacNewman, Howard Mandelbaum, Marian Malatesta, Loïcia Margotat, Chris Marino, Bill Martinez, Scott McAlister, Martha McClintock, Rose McLendon, Brenna McCormick-Thompson, Susan McElrath, Gina McGinn, Lynn Maliszewski, Lesley Martin, Tony Mastres, Brenna McCormick-Thompson, Megan McKinney, Lisa Masengale, Augustus Mayhew, Sally Meakin, Elizabeth Maura Mescher, Sue Mendez, Anne Marie Menta, Erica Meyer, Philip Meza, Arthur H. Miller, Jason Miller, Angela Moore, Christina Moretta, Angela Morris, Allan Morrison, Jean Moulin, Steven Emlaw Murphy, Steffani Murray, Anuja Navare, Emily Newell, Emmie Nillson, Barbara Nitzberg, Juergen Nogai, Scott Norman, John Notz, Jr., Benjamin Nyholm, Suzanne Oatey, Liz O'Brien, Meg Ocampo, Katie O'Connell, Matt Ogden, John Olsen, Debra Orellana, Janet Owen, Mitchell Owens, Albert Palacios, Barbara Paquette, Judith Paquette, Nathaniel Parks, Laura Parrish, Christopher Parsons, Thad Partridge, Prof. Randall Patton, Mary Pedraza, Kent Penwell, Carol Peterson, Debra Peterson, Jennifer Pfaff, Julie Pierotti, Marc Porcher, Kevin Polglase, Katy Polsby, Terri Lynn Pond, Liza Posas, Michelle Press, Suzie Provo, Joel Puliatti, Ann Pyne, Kris Quist, Marton Radkai, Sandy Rauschhuber, Miles Redd, Ada Regan, Reproductions, Inc., Rev.com, John Rexine, Suzanne Rheinstein, Deborah Rice, David Rice, Hugh and Lesa Rider, Katie Ridder, Jane Roland, Barbara Rominski, Sylvia Rowan, Penny Rozis, Lisa Rubens, William Rutledge, Joseph Ryan, Mary Saenz, Suzanne Sakai, Jeremy Salloum, John Sanders, Davis Sandys, Gil Schafer, Susie Schang, Peter Schifando, Anne Schnoebelen, Karen Schoenberg, Clarrie Scholtz, Tracey Schuster, Kathryn Sellers, Sharon's Cottage Quilts, Adrienne Sharpe-Weseman, Sarah Sherman Clark, David Silverman, Dawn Sims, Jess Smith, Kristin N. Smith, Natalie Snoyman, Jeanne Solensky, Laurie Stein, Karen Stern, Norman and Norah Stone, Jon Sturtevant, Michael Sturtevant, Tami Suzuki, Jenny Swadosh, Sally Swing, Julia Tanenbaum, Eve Steccati Tanovitz, Gayle Tantau, Cordes Tarantino, Killian Taylor, Springer Teich, Andrug Tenwang, Jeff Thomas, Alecia Thomas, Shan Thomas, Anne Thomason, Faye Thompson, Sirie Thongchua, Martha Thorne, Laurel Thornton, Marcia Tingley, Robin Toolin, Lisa Tranks, Kathy Trafton, Emily Tran-Le, Helaine Tregenza, G.Tregouet, Terry and Paula Trotter, Dan Trujillo, Eric Van der Wyk, Carleton Varney, Jan Venturini, Mark Vieira, Christopher Voss, Inge Waite, Jay Walkinshaw, Theo Walther, Marc Wanamaker, Phyllis Washington, Nancy Webster, Gloria Weltz, Emily Una Weirich, Donald West, Marcelle White, Maggie Wickenden, Susan Wilke, Amy Williams, Tim Wilson, Kay Wisniewski, Martin Wood, Ashlee Wright, Brenda Galloway-Wright, Richard Wright, Sheila Yates, Norman Yee, Russ Young, Timothy Young (Beinecke Library, Yale University, Jee Young Kim (Tony Duquette Inc.), Ray Youngdahl, Joe Yranski, Cynthia Ziegler, and Russell Zimmerman.

I have been researching and reporting on Frances Elkins for more than two decades and inevitably I may have overlooked the superb assistance and kindness of a source whose insight or knowledge I truly appreciate.•

PHOTOGRAPHY CREDITS

117. (top) Courtesy of the Roger Sturtevant Collection, Oakland Museum of California. Gift of Roger Sturtevant; (bottom) Al Ruschmeyer.
118. Raymond W. Trowbridge photo, Scott Powell collection.
119. Raymond W. Trowbridge photo, Scott Powell collection.
120. Raymond W. Trowbridge photo, Scott Powell collection.
121. (top) Raymond W. Trowbridge photo, Scott Powell collection; (bottom) Raymond W. Trowbridge photo, Scott Powell collection.
122-23. Raymond W. Trowbridge photo, Scott Powell collection.
124. Emelie Danielson, courtesy of David S. Boyd.
125. (left) Emelie Danielson, courtesy of David S. Boyd; (right) Emelie Danielson, Scott Powell collection
126. (top) Luis Medina/*Architectural Digest* © 1980/Condé Nast Publications, Inc.; (bottom) Robert Brost photo, courtesy of William E. Boyd..
127. Emelie Danielson, courtesy of David S. Boyd.
128-29. Emelie Danielson, courtesy of David S. Boyd.
129 (top) Jared Goss; (bottom) Robert Brost photo, courtesy of William E. Boyd.
130. (top) Emelie Danielson, courtesy of David S. Boyd; (bottom) Jared Goss.
131. Luis Medina, David Adler Collection, Ryerson and Burnham Art and Architecture Archives, Art Institute of Chicago.
132. Emelie Danielson, Scot Powell collection.
133. (top) Luis Medina, David Adler Collection, Ryerson and Burnham Art and Architecture Archives, Art Institute of Chicago; (bottom) *House & Garden* © 1951/Condé Nast Publications, Inc.
134. (top) Luis Medina, David Adler Collection, Ryerson and Burnham Art and Architecture Archives, Art Institute of Chicago; (bottom) Emelie Danielson, Scott Powell collection.
135. (top left) Jared Goss; (top right) Luis Medina, David Adler Collection, Ryerson and Burnham Art and Architecture Archives, Art Institute of Chicago; (bottom) Robert Brost photo, courtesy of William E. Boyd.
136. (top) Luis Medina/*Architectural Digest* © 1980/Condé Nast Publications, Inc.; (bottom) Emelie Danielson, Scott Powell collection.
137. Emelie Danielson, Courtesy of Frances Adler Elkins Collection, Monterey Peninsula College Library Archives & Special Collections Department.
138-139. © Jess Smith/PHOTOSMITH.
139. (top) © Jess Smith/PHOTOSMITH; (bottom) Courtesy of Stephen Bent.
140-41. Jim Bartsch.
142-43. Jim Bartsch.
144-45. Jim Bartsch.
146. (top) Jim Bartsch; (bottom) Jim Bartsch.
147. (top) Jim Bartsch; (bottom) Scott Powell.
148. (all) Robert Brost photo, courtesy of William E. Boyd.
149. Peter Nyholm/*Vogue* © 1936 Condé Nast Publications, Inc.
150. Robert Brost photo, courtesy of William E. Boyd.
151. (top) Robert Brost photo, courtesy of William E. Boyd; (bottom) Courtesy of Frances Adler Elkins Collection, Monterey Peninsula College Library Archives & Special Collections Department.
152. (all) Robert Brost photos, courtesy of William E. Boyd.
153. Peter Nyholm/*Vogue* © 1936 Condé Nast Publications, Inc.
154. André Kertész/ *House & Garden* © 1946 Condé Nast Publications, Inc.
155. Robert Brost photo, courtesy of William E. Boyd.
156-57. Julian P. Graham, courtesy of Harry Hunt, Jr.
158. Julian P. Graham photos / Pebble Beach Co. Lagorio Archive;
159. Trotter Galleries.
160-161 Ezra Stoller © Esto. All rights reserved.
162-163. (all) Robert Brost photos, courtesy of William E. Boyd.
164-165. (all) Robert Brost photos, courtesy of William E. Boyd.
166-67. (all) © Fred Lyon, courtesy of Barbara Gardner and Kitty Margolis.
168-69. (all) The Suffolk County Vanderbilt Museum, Centerpoint, New York.
170-71. Maynard L. Parker, photographer. Courtesy of The Huntington Library, San Marino, California.
172-73. Maynard L. Parker, photographer. Courtesy of The Huntington Library, San Marino, California
174. Max Heinegg, Courtesy of Frances Adler Elkins Collection, Monterey Peninsula College Library Archives & Special Collections Department.

175. Max Heinegg, courtesy of Susan Zellerbach.
176. (top) Max Heinegg, courtesy of Susan Zellerbach; (bottom) Max Heinegg, courtesy of Susan Zellerbach.
177. (top) Mark Sinclair, courtesy of Stephen M. Salny; (bottom) © Fred Lyon.
178. Max Heinegg, courtesy of Norman Stone.
179. (both) Max Heinegg, courtesy of Susan Zellerbach.
180. Courtesy of the Morse / Osborne family archives.
181. Scott Powell.
182. (top) Maynard L. Parker, photographer. Courtesy of The Huntington Library, San Marino, California; (bottom) Russell MacMasters.
183. Maynard L. Parker, photographer. Courtesy of The Huntington Library, San Marino, California.
184. (both) Roger Sturtevant, The William W. Wurster/ WBE collection, UC Berkeley Environmental Design Archives.
185. (top) Courtesy of David S. Boyd; (bottom) Courtesy of the Roger Sturtevant Collection, Oakland Museum of California. Gift of Roger Sturtevant.
186. (top) Courtesy of David S. Boyd; (bottom) Dorothy Liebes Papers, Archives of American Art, Smithsonian Institution.
187. Dorothy Liebes Papers, Archives of American Art, Smithsonian Institution.
188-89. Courtesy of David S. Boyd; colorization by Victor Mascaro.
189. (right) Roger Sturtevant, The William W. Wurster/ WBE collection, UC Berkeley Environmental Design Archives.
190-91. Courtesy of David S. Boyd; colorization by Victor Mascaro.
191. (right) Roger Sturtevant, The William W. Wurster/ WBE collection, UC Berkeley Environmental Design Archives.
192. Courtesy of Diane Bower.
194. (left) Courtesy of Jayne Gasperson; (right) Scott Powell collection.
195. (top) Philip Fein, courtesy of David S. Boyd; (bottom) Philip Fein, courtesy of David S. Boyd.
196. (top left) photo by U.S. Army Signal Corps., W.T. Lee & Co.; (bottom left) photo by U.S. Army Signal Corps, W.T. Lee & Co.; (right) Courtesy of David S. Boyd.
197. (both) © Harrison Memorial Library, Carmel, CA. [
198. (top left) Dorothy Liebes Papers, Archives of American Art, Smithsonian Institution; (top right) Dorothy Liebes Papers, Archives of American Art, Smithsonian Institution; (bottom left) Dorothy Liebes Papers, Archives of American Art, Smithsonian Institution; (bottom right) Courtesy of Frances Adler Elkins Collection, Monterey Peninsula College Library Archives & Special Collections Department.
199. San Francisco Museum of Modern Art Library & Archives.
200. (top left) Russell MacMasters; (top right) Maynard L. Parker photo, *House Beautiful*, October 1590, courtesy of *House Beautiful*/Hearst Magazine Media, Inc.; (bottom) Russell MacMasters.
201. Courtesy of Chris Bunn.
202-203. Courtesy of the Roger Sturtevant Collection, Oakland Museum of California. Gift of Roger Sturtevant.
204-205. Adler Arts Center and Stephen M. Salny
206. (both) Roger Sturtevant, Gardner A. Dailey Collection, UC Berkeley Environmental Design Archives.
207. (top) Courtesy of Lee Jofa and DecoratorsBest; (bottom) Courtesy of the Roger Sturtevant Collection, Oakland Museum of California. Gift of Roger Sturtevant.
208-209. Roger Sturtevant, courtesy of David S. Boyd.
210-211. (all) Roger Sturtevant, The William W. Wurster/ WBE collection, UC Berkeley Environmental Design Archives.
212. Courtesy of David S. Boyd.
213. Maynard L. Parker, photographer. Courtesy of The Huntington Library, San Marino, California,
214-215. Maynard L. Parker, photographer. Courtesy of The Huntington Library, San Marino, California
216-217. Courtesy of David S. Boyd.
218. (top) Maynard L. Parker, photographer. Courtesy of The Huntington Library, San Marino, California; (bottom) Courtesy of David S. Boyd.
219. (top) Maynard L. Parker, photographer. Courtesy of The Huntington Library, San Marino, California; (bottom) Courtesy of David S. Boyd.
220. (top) Dorothy Liebes Papers, Archives of American Art, Smithsonian Institution; (bottom) Courtesy of the Roger Sturtevant Collection, Oakland Museum of California. Gift of Roger Sturtevant.

221. (top) Roger Sturtevant, Oakland Museum of California; (bottom) *San Francisco News-Call Bulletin* Photo Morgue, San Francisco History Center, San Francisco Public Library.
222. Courtesy of the Roger Sturtevant Collection, Oakland Museum of California. Gift of Roger Sturtevant.
223. Roger Sturtevant, courtesy of David S. Boyd.
224. (top) Roger Sturtevant, courtesy of David S. Boyd; (bottom) Philip Fein, courtesy of David S. Boyd.
225. (top) Courtesy of the Roger Sturtevant Collection, Oakland Museum of California. Gift of Roger Sturtevant; (bottom left) © Fred Lyon; (bottom right) © Fred Lyon.
226. (top) Roger Sturtevant, courtesy of David S. Boyd; (bottom) Courtesy of the Roger Sturtevant Collection, Oakland Museum of California. Gift of Roger Sturtevant.
227. Courtesy of the Roger Sturtevant Collection, Oakland Museum of California. Gift of Roger Sturtevant
228. © Yousuf Karsh.
229. Courtesy of the Roger Sturtevant Collection, Oakland Museum of California. Gift of Roger Sturtevant.
230. © Fred Lyon, *House & Garden* 1949/Condé Nast Publications, Inc.
231. Philip Fein, UC Berkeley Environmental Design Archives
232. © Fred Lyon.
233. © Fred Lyon.
234. (top) Courtesy of Frances Adler Elkins Collection, Monterey Peninsula College Library Archives & Special Collections Department; (bottom) Courtesy of David S. Boyd.
235. (top) Peter Breinig, courtesy of Jim Costello; (bottom) California History Room, Monterey Public Library.
236-237: Maynard L. Parker, photographer. Courtesy of The Huntington Library, San Marino, California.
238: (two left images) Maynard L. Parker, photographer. Courtesy of The Huntington Library, San Marino, California.
238-239. Scott Powell collection.
240-241. Maynard L. Parker, photographer. Courtesy of The Huntington Library, San Marino, California
242-243. Maynard L. Parker, photographer. Courtesy of The Huntington Library, San Marino, California
244. Julius Shulman, Getty Research Institute, Los Angeles (2004.R.10), © J. Paul Getty Trust.
245. © Fred Lyon.
246. (top) Julius Shulman/*House & Garden* © 1952/Condé Nast Publications, Inc.; (bottom left) Julius Shulman/ *House & Garden* © 1952/Condé Nast Publications, Inc.; (bottom right) © Fred Lyon.
247. Julius Shulman/*House & Garden* © 1952/Condé Nast Publications, Inc.
248-249. Fred Lyon/*House & Garden* © 1948/Condé Nast Publications, Inc.
250. Fred Lyon/*House & Garden* © 1947/Condé Nast Publications, Inc.
251. (left) Fred Lyon/*House & Garden* © 1948/Condé Nast Publications, Inc.; (right) all photos by Slim Aarons/Getty Images.
252-53. Philip Fein, courtesy of David S. Boyd.
254. (top) Philip Fein, Courtesy of Frances Adler Elkins Collection, Monterey Peninsula College Library Archives & Special Collections Department; (bottom) Philip Fein, courtesy of David S. Boyd.
255. © Fred Lyon.
256. Maynard L. Parker, photographer. Courtesy of The Huntington Library, San Marino, California.
257. The William W. Wurster/WBE collection, UC Berkeley Environmental Design Archives.
258-259. Moulin Studios photos, courtesy of Frances Adler Elkins Collection, Monterey Peninsula College Library Archives & Special Collections Department.
260-61. Roger Sturtevant, Gardner A. Dailey Collection, UC Berkeley Environmental Design Archives.
262-63. Roger Sturtevant, Gardner A. Dailey Collection, UC Berkeley Environmental Design Archives.
264-265. (black and white) Roger Sturtevant, Gardner A. Dailey Collection, UC Berkeley Environmental Design Archives.
264-265. (color) Roger Sturtevant, courtesy of Barbara Gardner.
266-67. Philip Fein, courtesy of Stephen M. Salny and Milton Johnson.
268. Scott Powell.
270. San Francisco Museum of Modern Art Library & Archives.
271. (top) Roger Sturtevant, Gardner A. Dailey Collection, UC Berkeley Environmental Design Archives; (bottom)

First published in the United States of America in 2023 by
Rizzoli International Publications, Inc.
300 Park Avenue South
New York, NY 10010
www.rizzoliusa.com

Copyright © 2023 Scott Powell

Publisher: Charles Miers
Editor: Ellen Nidy
Design: Sarah Gifford
Production Manager: Colin Hough Trapp
Managing Editor: Lynn Scrabis

Printed in China

2023 2024 2025 2026 2027 / 10 9 8 7 6 5 4 3 2 1

ISBN: 978-0-8478-6546-8

Library of Congress Control Number: 2023977683

Visit us online:
Facebook.com / RizzoliNewYork
instagram.com/rizzolibooks
twitter.com/Rizzoli_Books
pinterest.com/rizzolibooks
youtube.com/user/RizzoliNY
issuu.com/rizzoli

PAGE 2 Colonial-flavored north living room
as seen from the south living room (aka the
"lounge"), Shoreacres Country Club (Lake
Bluff, Illinois), circa 1924.

PAGES 4–5 Bar and adjoining card room,
James D. Zellerbach house, decorated
1937. The wall paneling and furniture were
designed by Frances, influenced by Jean-
Michel Frank.